THE DANCE HAS MANY FACES

The Dance Has Many Faces

SECOND EDITION

EDITED BY

WALTER SORELL

Columbia
University Press
New York
& London

17014

Frontispiece:

Doris Humphrey at rehearsal with Ruth Currier
Photo by Radford Bascome; courtesy of Ruth Currier

Louis Horst, teacher, composer, spiritual guide of
three generations of modern dancers
Collection Walter Sorell

Copyright 1951 by Walter Sorell
Copyright © 1966 by Columbia University Press

First Edition published by The World Publishing Company 1951
Second Edition published by Columbia University Press 1966
Second printing 1968

Library of Congress Catalog Card Number: 66-25457
Printed in the United States of America

To the memory
of those who were dear and close to me
DORIS HUMPHREY and LOUIS HORST

Acknowledgments

I wish to express my sincerest gratitude for the kindness and cooperation with which my new contributors have assisted me and have made a dream come true twice.

My thanks go to the editors of *Dance Magazine* for permission to reprint Alwin Nikolais' "Growth of a Theme," which he has extended for this edition, also to use George Jackson's "Native in Its Naked Beauty," which he has adapted to *The Living Dolls*, and for permission to condense the three articles of "Pauline Koner Speaking"; the editors of *Criticism* for excerpts of Selma Jeanne Cohen's essay "Avant-Garde Choreography"; the editors of *It Is* for Merle Marsicano's feature "Thoughts on Dance"; the *Dance Observer* for permission to use some of the material published in their issues; "New York" the Sunday *Herald Tribune* for Walter Terry's "Favorable Balance of Trade"; *Dance Index* for John Martin's "Dance on Film"; to Mr. Enrico Fulchignoni, Chef de la section des films culturels, United Nations Educational Organization, for permitting me to edit Birgit Cullberg's speech delivered during the International Congress on Dance, Ballet and Pantomime in Television and Films at Salzburg in August 1965; to Boosey and Hawkes, Inc., who authorized the inclusion of an example from the score of Stravinsky's *Apollon Musagète*.

A Note

THE DANCE HAS MANY FACES which I edited in 1951 has been out of print for many years and now, thanks to Columbia University Press, re-emerges with many new faces. Some of the essays did not find their way back into this edition, not because I want to disavow them but because time has passed them by. In the arts, more so than in life, time has a merciless way of keeping step with nothing and no one.

Fifteen years have elapsed. Since then many new problems have become urgent, and some of the older questions more problematic. Certain topics are ageless and remained so while the history made for a day or two whizzed by. Certain ideas stood well the test of time. In some cases I felt that a new face (even though it may have the graying temples of maturity) now expresses better what is of interest to us. In other cases I asked the same contributors to rewrite their essays, aligning them with the contemporary point of view.

Every anthologist faces the problem of choice. But often it has been a difficult one since I dealt with dancers and, in most cases, with not yet written material. (I have learned to love them despite all their idiosyncrasies, the "lonewolves" as well as those "cocoon-enveloped" and "I-am-different-from-you" personalities.) In a sense, this anthology is like a show, and I as producer have had to replace some faces—still dear to me—and accept a compromise here and there, fully aware that it is a compromise. In this greatly revised book I feel far less the almost unavoidable discrepancy between the envisioned and the performed. In the main, I find the dancer-choreographer of our days very articulate, verbally as much as physically. I have also added the voices of some critics, but restricted them to the role of historians.

Many faces can be seen again between these covers, united in their diversity, trying to serve one cause: the dance.

WALTER SORELL

Contents

THE DANCE OF TODAY AND TOMORROW / 209

Illustrations

THE DANCE HAS MANY FACES

*... Dancing as an art, we may be sure,
cannot die out, but will always be undergoing a rebirth. Not merely as
an art, but also as a social custom, it perpetually emerges afresh from
the soul of the people ...*   —HAVELOCK ELLIS

LA MERI

The Ethnological Dance Arts

THE TERM "ethnological dance" is one which has sprung
up within the last decade and is applied, loosely, to all
the racial and ethnic dance forms of all the peoples of
the world. The title is a cumbersome one, as I should know
very well since I have worked in its shadow for many years.
"Ethnological dancers" specializing in one style only, are called
"Spanish dancers" or "Hindu dancers" or, at most, "Oriental
dancers"; but my own talent has lain not in the further perfection of a single form but in breadth of interpretation of the
bodies, techniques, psychologies and souls of the many peoples
of East and West alike. This type of study engenders a great
tolerance which is often mistaken for lack of dedication; while
technical ease and a deep, personal love for the peoples represented give to the uninitiated the impression that the dancer is
"tossing it off." This is a grave error brought about by the Western habit of thinking. We have come to consider the word
"technique" as applicable only to the movements which are so
showy as to approach acrobacy: leaps, turns, extensions, etc. The
term actually applies also to the arms, hands, head and expres-

sions in any type of dance, and it is an error to applaud the technique of a ballarino if his legs are good but his arms bad. The *aficionado* of the Spanish dance seldom employs the word "technique." It is too all-embracing to be used casually. He says that Argentina's castanets are without equal; that Pastora Imperio's *brazeo* (arm-carriage) is divine. And he is fully aware that technique is useless unless it is put at the service of emotionalism. In the oriental dance the whole focus of attention changes. The technical vehicle of the emotionalism is the *upper body* culminating in the hands and face. The lower body is the accompaniment to the melody of the upper body. But rare indeed is the Western critic (or audience) who can re-focus his attention to properly watch the Eastern dance. And the *punkhita* (trembling) hand like the Spanish castanets does not look difficult, and so its mastery evokes no applause, either manual or printed, such as accompanies the execution of the thirty-two pirouettes. And let me parenthesis here and now that the great ballarinas are *not* deluded by ease of execution into believing that the exotic techniques are easy!

Strictly speaking, the ethnological dance does not include the folk dance, the former being an art dance and the latter a communal dance. But I believe it is safe to say that all ethnological dance arts spring from communal dance.

Hindu Natya, which is the most complete dance science alive today, sprung from communal worship. The *hasta-mudras* (hand poses) which form the basis of the Hindu dance originated as a ritual in the chanting of the Rig-Vedic hymns. At first only the priests used these mudras—much as the Catholic priest or Jewish rabbi uses ritualistic gestures. The high priest alone was aware of the esoteric meanings, but the exoteric meaning was one which illustrated the words of the hymns. A later development was the devadasi—the temple dancer, whose function was not unlike that of the occidental choir singer, save that the former "danced" with her hands instead of singing, or while singing. During the glory of the Vijayanagara Empire, the kings—great patrons of the temple arts—raised the art of the devadasi to a far greater perfection, and paved the way for its eventual branching into secularization. It was at this time that the nrtta (pure dance) developed, adding as interlude to the nrttya (pantomimic) passages, both steps and mudras which had no function beyond that of mere decoration. It is said in South India that since the fall of the Vijayanagara Empire, Bharata Natyam has deteriorated; but to those of us fortunate enough to have seen it performed, it remains a great and perfect dance science. Still used in the temples where it was born, today it also knows the concert stage.

The story of Bharata Natyam—its slow growth over the centuries with roots in the very heart of the Hindu religion and every branch, flower and fruit the loving work of the people of the land—is the typical story of all the true ethnological dance arts.

The indigenous Japanese dance is a refinement of the indigenous folk dance, and to these forms have been added the arts of China and India when the techniques of these two great countries had already evolved from communal to art forms.

The delicate theater dance of Java is a combination of the imported Hindu technique superimposed on the purely Javanese ancestor-worship rituals.

Bali's dance art is still a communal affair, her greatest artists being simple members of a community where *all* dance. And in Ceylon the devil dancers are mostly farmers who have inherited from their fathers the right to perform ritualistic dances whose technique is definitely South Indian.

The Burmese dance drama was imported from Siam during the years of Burma's dominance over that country. But the true Burmese dance, that of the "posture girls" which precedes the dramas, is a combination of the communal Pwe and the ritualistic dances to the thirty-seven "nats"—the gods of pre-Buddhistic days.

Nearer to their communal origines are the choreographies of

the Occident. The Spanish dance, whose great antiquity cannot be questioned, has many facets in its folk expression. From the north come the dances whose roots lie in the dark earth of ancient fertility rites. From the central Mesa come dances which have passed rapidly from the fields through the court to the theater. From the south come dances of the *sudras* of India (flamencos), of the Moors and of the soil. From the east come dances of pyrrhic origin, and Egypt and Phoenicia likewise have left their mark on the choreographies of Iberia. But it is within the last century that this eclectic dance has been combined into an art form which can take its place beside the theater art of Java or Japan. For dance dramas have been written, choreographed and executed in the pure idiom of the Spanish dance, and today tradition is being crystallized.

The Polynesian dances are still communal at home. It is with their transplantation abroad that they are becoming "theater." And now, indeed, is the crucial moment of unfolding for this naive and beautiful idiom. It is in need of a great native artist who will move it out of the cabarets and into the concert halls: to do for it what Argentina did for the Spanish dance.

There is often a great danger in the passage from a folk expression to an art form. Emasculation may lie between. The Scotch dances were born as the emotional expression of a bold and warlike peoples. Not many years ago I saw them done by the Gordon Highlanders. It was the most thoroughly exciting performance I have ever witnessed. But what of the passage of this dance towards the academization of artistry? One sees girls of twelve, hung with the medals of past awards, executing reel, fling and sword dance in virginal ballet slippers—*battement*, trained toes beating slim calves with careful precision. But is this the Scotch dance? God forbid! For the breath of life has gone out of it and it has forgotten why it was born.

One day in my Spanish class I suddenly realized that at the

earnest badgering of certain of my pupils, I had been for some months teaching *steps* with painful precision; and that all these steps had not led to the execution of a single copla of the Sevillanas! I tried in an impassioned speech to my gaping students to explain my feelings, my violated principles—and I sailed out of the classroom registering the vow that I *never again* would teach, via the route of precise technique, a dance whose very essence lies in its emotional fathering.

For the ethnologic dance is not a product of the mind but of the emotions. Style is its essence, but technique, as we are all too prone to understand it, is of purely relative importance. Neither Argentina nor Argentinita ever executed a double vuelta-quebrada; and, if they did or did not, it would have had no bearing on their value as artists. Technique—bodily control—must be mastered *only* because the body must not stand in the way of the soul's expression.

It is my opinion that all ethnologic dance arts are the slow processing of the communal dance. I do not believe that a dance art can be expressive of a certain people unless it is the product of a cross section of that people. The ballet is not an ethnologic dance because it is the result of the work of Italy, France, Spain and Russia. As such it cannot represent fully any one of the four. By the same reasoning the American modern dance is the product of individuals, and not of the American people. We cannot hurry the production of art as we do the assembly line. I do not doubt that with the passing of the years, nay, of the centuries, the American moderns will have made their contribution to our country's dance. But we cannot afford to disregard the jitterbug, whose expression is an exact parallel of the flamenco. Both gitano and "rug-cutter" beat the floor in ecstatic counter-rhythms to satisfy an inner emotional urge, little aware of the effect on those who watch him. One hundred years ago the average cultured Spaniard felt toward the flamenco dance much as many cultured Americans

feel toward jive, et al. But today flamenco is a recognized and beloved art both at home and abroad, and has been fused with the
Andalusian dance to produce the neo-classic dance art of Spain.
Here lies a lesson which we cannot afford to disregard. For it has
always been, and will always be the emotional experience of the
folk of the race which is the backbone of the country's ethnologic art.

The teaching of ethnologic dance, if properly done, requires
a good deal more from teacher and pupils alike than might be
supposed. In India the *guru* (teacher) is said to have far more
influence than have the parents on the growth and formation of
the pupil's character. For the study of the dances of the East
entails not only the mastery of physical techniques, but of spiritual and psychological growth. Without a knowledge and understanding of the culture, the religion, the folkways which give
birth to the art, it is impossible to perform that art. This is
equally true of the dance of Spain, Polynesia and other Occidental
lands. If *guru* and pupil are natives, backgrounds and social habits
are relatively identical and there is no need to begin by building a bridge of understanding. If the *guru* is native and pupil
foreign, then the latter must have a great knowledge, a great instinct, or both, to ferret out and analyze the essential bodily,
spiritual and psychological differences between his own culture
and that of his teacher. If both *guru* and pupil are foreign to the
art with which they work, then the *guru* must carefully and *individually* resolve a system of disclosing to the pupil, step by step,
the thousand subtle differences in the emanation and physical
reactions of the native and the foreigner. If the pupil is young,
open-minded and brings to his study a great love, a great desire
and an unquestioning respect, the way is possible. But the pit-
falls are many and to the *guru* each pupil presents a different psychological problem.

The physical techniques vary from race to race and from

country to country. They are conditioned by the clothes worn, the ground walked on, the manner of sitting and bowing and worshipping, the physical characteristics of the people. The base of ethnological characterization is the backbone. Without a control of the spine-line so perfect that it has become instinctive, it is impossible to interpret the dances of Japan or of Spain. I have named these as examples because the spine-line of the two differs so widely. The most sensuous part of the Japanese feminine body is the back of the neck, but the Spanish woman lifts her breasts proudly upward.

The spine-line is just the beginning. Each part of the body has a different characteristic from country to country. Toes turn in in Japan, forward in Burma, out in Java. Feminine thighs cling, masculine spread in nearly all forms of ethnic dance, since there is a deeply felt consciousness of sex in all ethnological forms. (For this reason psychotherapeutists claim these forms to be healthier psychologically than ballet or modern.) In Java feminine upper arms cling to the body, masculine lift outward; and in Spain upper arms arch upward. Hands—which in all humanity are so revealing—show widely differing traits from country to country; and all over the East, the manual technique is the keynote of choreography. The carriage of the head is a part of the spine-line, but characteristic neck movements show throughout the Orient. And what of the face? Here we have the subtlest technique of all, for emotional expression must ripple like an undercurrent beneath the masklike face of Siam or China; and a lamp must be lit behind the fabulously complicated muscular *mukhaja* (face technique) of India.

Few indeed are the foreigners capable of judging the ethnological dance beyond the point of an instinctive aesthetic reaction to a great beauty. And because in many forms of ethnic dance the art carries the artist, the strangeness and strength of the art itself is believed to be the strength of the artist.

Inversely, once the strangeness has worn off, the watcher (or critic) reaches that no man's land between instinctive reaction and knowledgeable judgment and is quite incapable of seeing the inner qualities of the individual artist. By inner qualities I mean the good points—such as expressive hands, controlled toes, sincere emotionalism—which might be momentarily overshadowed by such drawbacks as youth, inexpertness, or even momentary difficulties such as a bad stage or poorly played music. The knife cuts two ways. A watcher, accustomed all his life to ballet, applauds vigorously the "technique" of a young ethnological dancer although that dancer *locks* his knees, which in this field is a technical error as grave as loose knees in ballet. But we are accustomed to certain lines and we loudly condemn all others. We have not yet learned (with the Javanese) that the cultured person is possessed of humility and lowers his eyes; that only the vulgar go through life with round, staring eyes and open mouth.

The ethnological dance is the product of the necessity for pure emotional expression. Even the casual observer will concede this point to the Spanish dance. Purely emotional from egotistic castanets to sadistic heels and sexually aware in every line and movement of both masculine and feminine body, it has no reason to exist at all without the driving strength of emotional pressure behind it. But the Javanese dance is not less the product of the necessity for emotional expression. Here again we must not think the emotional level of all people is identical with our own. We, like the Spaniard, must "spit it out," "get it off the chest." But the Easterner must rise above, must seek Brahmananda. And can you watch the Javanese dance without feeling a strange, new calm envelop you? This is a choreography with an unequaled power, for it carries a quasi-hypnotism in which watcher and dancer seem to leave themselves behind, and lift their astral bodies to move in some suspended place between heaven and earth. But we are afraid of this hypnotism, and we squeeze our eyes shut like frightened children and whine, "I don't like it! It isn't exciting!" It *is* exciting; but exciting on a far

the Thursday evening service. One night, right in the middle of attempting to visualize some particular Psalm, I suddenly had a brain wave. I left the group sitting on the floor where we had been discussing the possible form for the Psalm, and dashed downstairs. To my delight I found Meri at the end of her class. I begged her to come up to my studio, convinced as I was that she had a great contribution to make to my Temple work. I knew that the moment had come for us to study her *hasta-mudras* in order to utilize, in a more translated manner, this universal speech of the hands. The Choir followed her gestures and explanations in open-mouthed wonder as she revealed to them what she had to me, a marvelous new means of expression.

Alas, I fear that we have not been very scholarly or faithful to the vision she gave us that night, but we are still stumbling along. As a group we profited aesthetically by her teachings, while I personally have been refreshed and released by my attempts to translate the rich sonorous phrases of the Psalms into a kind of *hasta-mudra* for the West. I also have done a number of my own poems in this way. But what is most important, my students have been trained in a new medium for interpreting the Lord's Prayer, the Doxology and many of the sublime Psalms. I still feel that we are mere beginners. But whatever we have accomplished, or may accomplish in the future, we place to the credit of La Meri for her aesthetic and spiritual fusion of East and West.

As we continue our specialized application of the *mudras*, I find there are, roughly, two phases of adaptation. One needs but a free and beautifully lyrical movement of the whole body, with the hands used only in a decorative and expressive manner. The other definitely requires the specific language of the *hasta-mudras*.

It is not my intention, nor was it Meri's when she gave us our initial inspiration, to limit our hand language to the Hindu. There are the Egyptian symbolic gestures, created of course by the priesthood for communicating Egyptian theology to the people. For centuries the Mass, our great Christian ritual, has had its authorized system of symbolic gestures which are well understood by the priesthood of the Catholic Church, but little known by the Protestants and other sects. It is our aim to use the *hasta-mudras* as a stimulus to exhaustive research in the language of the hand rather than to impose their specialized forms upon our culture. I am working upon a series of Psalms done both as plastic and as space-covering routines using a variety of hand gestures.

"The Cathedral of the Future" is my way of designating ideal conditions under which to explore the limitless possibilities of religious dance. Its construction must employ the entire range of modern architecture, scientific lighting and the use of materials characteristic of the age. Yet it should retain the dignity and functional adequacy of the magnificent religious structures of the past. I could go on endlessly describing details of such a cathedral but will limit myself to the few factors necessary for the greater expressiveness of celebrants and congregation.

First, it must be a "seeing" cathedral and not a mere "listening" one. The altar should be a wholly mobile place where the developing human spirit, making use of the total octave of arts, can reveal its changing and expanding consciousness. Objectively the altar should be a large circular area with a beautifully curved background capable of being lighted in a variety of effects. It must be harmoniously integrated into an auditorium assuring perfect visibility from every angle. Here in our studio-chapel we experimented one evening with what we called a "Litany of Arts." When this Litany brings into active focus all of the arts it will be the keynote of the Cathedral of the Future. Dance and drama, painting and sculpture, poetry and oratory, music and fine craftsmanship should enrich the consciousness of the celebrants, educate and inspire the congregation. Besides providing an avenue of self-expression for the minister and his officiating priests, the Cathedral of the Future must impel its communicants to spontaneous participation.

It is my entirely modest vision for this cathedral that its activities should more than rival contemporary offerings of stage and screen or their equivalent. Through a new pattern of audience-participation and the soul-satisfying dramas concerned with man himself rather than the constant comings and goings of his objective world, this dynamic center of wisdom and beauty should surpass in sheer attracting power any theater or other secular exposition of the arts. To state it briefly, I want to see the House of God the most fascinating and perfect creative center ever conceived, the flower of civilization.

To be sure the cathedrals of Europe fulfilled this ideal in many respects. But now, by virtue of our mechanical genius, we can quickly be transported from any given spot to somewhere else. Competing with the church there are theaters of various types, sports claiming national interest, men's and women's clubs of every description and a thousand other diversions to which our systems of rapid transit can take us. The result is that the unity of man is hourly disintegrated, because he *takes from without* instead of *giving from within*. The prime function of the Cathedral of the Future will be to promote his integration on a high level.

I wish to make it clear that I consider the great popular churches of today, with their allowed-for rumba dance halls, their ping-pong and bingo games, their social discussion groups where any current topic utterly unrelated to man's spiritual self-realization can occupy the excited oratory of their youth, as glaring examples of the church being invaded by the world instead of conquering it. Such activities may be a means of holding young people to membership, but they are among the disintegrating forces and bear no relationship to my ideal cathedral.

I do not expect to see this dream—miracles aside—brought

into manifestation in my time. But I do hope that some of our youth will be inspired to work on it from day to day and year to year so that a hundred or more years hence, leaning from the golden bar of heaven, I can be pleased and proud that seeds now being scattered have germinated and ultimately come to fruition.

———

DORIS HUMPHREY

Dance Drama

DANCE DRAMA began at the moment when the first man bridged the separated "I" and "you" with "tell." It began when the savage, bursting with the experience of his "I am," invented the first movements for telling a memory. Eons of movement and sound had existed before him in the animal kingdom, some of them as rhythmic and highly organized as a ballet. He himself had inherited all these movements and had developed many more in the process of becoming a man. But there came a day when a different feeling possessed him. The new element was the need to explain the emotional self, not just to feel it but to tell it to another. It must have come as a memory of experience, the difficult kill or the dangerous foray, after which the conscious "I" returned with a new desire, to communicate. There were, as yet, no words, so he described his adventures with movement and perhaps with sounds of the voice too. How could this have been a dance drama? Because it was rhythmic, it told a story, the body movements were dramatic, not realistic, and because it had an objective, an audience. That it was rhythmic, and not just pantomimic, seems beyond question. Our man, being close to nature, was bound up in her rhythmic structure, and besides, how could he have described running or walking without falling into a pattern? Constrained to stay within telling distance, these movements would fall into a beat, and as this is a pleasurable sensation, no doubt it was prolonged, especially if claps or sounds of appreciation came from the "you."

So it seems clear that dance dramas were the earliest conscious communications of men, antedating words, music, and all the other arts. This point would not be important, except that it emphasizes dance movement combined with dramatic feeling as fundamental in our culture, and that the age-old springs are in emotion, rhythm, and communication. Let all dancers and dramatists forget this at their peril! Deep in the bodies of men lie the memories of these things. Every man responds to rhythm, knows the feel of the killer and lover, and from these the primitive acts of running, leaping, striking, defending, grasping, tearing, relaxing, caressing, shouting; and his body remembers how to crawl with fear, burn with anger, ache with fatigue, kindle with power and success. Without these memories, even those which are moribund from over-civilization, there would be no dance drama today, or indeed any drama, for the rousing of action-memory in the onlooker, by whatever means, is the sole key to good theater. The most ancient and most direct appeal to the dramatic sense is through the art of the dance, the special inheritor of body experience, the container of every movement man has ever made.

The long ages passed; the simple dance of the savage became an elaborate ritual which was bound up with every thought and feeling in the life of the community. By 4000 B.C. many dance dramas in Egypt and other ancient lands took days to perform and exceeded in length and fervor anything of the sort that has followed. In every part of the world where men settled, they communicated with their gods through dance and related the stories of their race to each other with dance, music and poetry.

The height of the development seems to have been reached in the early Greek tragedy, with its chorus of singers and dancers. Slowly, however, the dancers lost their place of importance, not only in Greek tragedy but throughout the ensuing forms of culture. People continued to dance, nothing could stop so fundamental an urge, but no longer with the same high purpose, and the story is one of an unhappy decline throughout Europe. After the fall of Greece and Rome, the great darkness which engulfed the affairs of men extended likewise to the dance, and it was many centuries before any notable resurgence took place. When it did come, it was a re-doing of a pagan memory, for the Christian church frowned on the body with its life instinct for dramatic movement and would not countenance the dance.

Long after the gods had vanished and the new religion was well-established, people, at a loss for dramatic subject matter arising from their own lives, turned back to mythology and the glories of Greece with a nostalgic enthusiasm. This was the Renaissance which surged throughout Europe, permeating all cultural thought. Especially in the dance there was a great eruption of gods, goddesses, satyrs, fauns, nymphs, all set in the most elaborate dramatic form with massive production and orchestral score. Even the social life followed the pattern. Kings and Princes entertained with the help of the Bacchae and Eurydice, with Phaedra and Hippolytus. This era seemed poverty-stricken for original art stemming from the times, and illustrates, at least in the dance field, a yearning to be a part of a believed ritual expressed in action. An account of a social event of the times seems quaint and picturesque to us, yet how much of imagination and buoyancy is in it compared to the drabness of our own social affairs. The following ballet was performed at the marriage of Galeazzo Visconti, Duke of Milan, in 1489:

> The guests were led into the banquet hall where the table was bare. At the same time disguised figures entered the room through another door; Jason and the Argonauts appeared in war attire, did homage to the newly weds, and spread the Golden Fleece as a covering over the table. Then Mercury appeared; he

had stolen the fatted calf from Apollo and everybody danced around the Golden Calf. To the sounds of the horns, Diana and her nymphs brought in Actaeon, transformed into a stag, and congratulated him on his good fortune in being eaten by Isabella, the ducal bride. Orpheus carried in the birds which he had caught when, charmed by his song, they had come too near. Theseus and Atalanta hunted the Calydonian boar in a wild dance, and proffered their captive in a triumphant round. Iris in her chariot brought the peacocks, Tritons served the fish, and Hebe with the Arcadian shepherds, Vertumna and Pomona, nectar and dessert. After the meal, Orpheus appeared with Hymen and the gods of love. Connubial Faith, brought in by the Graces, presented herself to the Duchess, but was interrupted by Semiramis, Helen, Phaedra, Medea, and Cleopatra, singing the charms of unfaithfulness. Connubial Faith ordered them out and the goddesses of love threw themselves with torches upon the Queens. Whereupon Lucretia, Penelope, Thomyris, Judith, Portia and Sulpicia laid out at the feet of the Duchess the palms which they had earned by a life of chastity, and, rather unexpectedly, Bacchus, Silenus and the satyrs appeared to conclude the ballet with a lively dance.

Very shortly after this period the dance drama was to enter another decline, as the great dramatists, composers and poets began to take over the drama and the stage. Also there was the Church. The two together combined to overwhelm the dance drama for several hundred years and to reduce it to a pretty interlude in an opera, or a ballroom scene in a play. Partly, too, this was due to the durability of the play-script and the musical score; the word and the musical sign could be transferred, sent on a journey intact, studied, criticized, while the dance suffered from its evanescence. When the curtain came down the play-script was still in the hands of the prompter, while the dance was locked in the bodies of the dancers. The Church, too, chose the dance as a special target of condemnation. This was logical, given the premise that the spirit could reach divine grace only by purification of the vile and degenerate body. Therefore anything which tended to glorify the body must be banned, and theologians strove mightily to uproot and cast out that evil thing, the dance. A vivid description of this attitude is afforded by a Puritan, one Phillip Stebbes in his *Anatomie of Abuses*, written in 1538. It recounts, not the iniquities of the stage, which was a favorite subject, but something in his mind much worse, a celebration in which he detects the stench of paganism.

> Against May, Whitsonday, or other time, all the young men and maides, older men and wives, run gadding over night to the woods, groves, hils and mountains, where they spend all the night in pleasant pastimes; and in the morning they return, bringing with them birch and branches of trees, to deck their assemblies withall. And no mervaile, for there is a great Lord present amongst them, as superintendent and Lord over their pastimes and sportes, namely Sathan, prince of hel. But the chiefest jewel they bring from thence is their May-Pole (this stinking ydol, rather) which is covered all over with floures and hearbs. And then fall they to daunce about it, like as the heathen people did at the dedication of the ydols, whereof this is a perfect pattern, or rather, the thing itself.

This May-Day celebration was a relic of a prehistoric fertility rite, originally a communication to the tree spirit. Mr. Stebbes was right about the origin, it was pagan, but he did not know that the religious significance was lost, and he could not know the innocent urge of people to make merry together in the dance. Civilized people do not believe in tree spirits any more, yet the May-Pole dance survives the Puritans and all other vicissitudes and is performed to this day all over Europe and North America, one of the few remaining communal dance dramas.

One outstanding exception to the exclusion of the dance by the Church existed a little later than Puritan days and deserves mention. The followers of the Shaker faith, or more properly the Society of True Believers, led by Mother Ann Lee, emigrated to the United States from England in the early nineteenth century. After establishing colonies here, they invented a ritual of which dance was a welcome and important part. Their ceremonies also aimed at purifying the body, in common with general Christian principles, but they came to the unique conclusion that this could be done better with the dance than without it, a conception which has yet to be adopted generally with any conspicuous success. The Shaker ritual met all definitions for great dance drama. It had a lofty purpose, it was dramatic, communicative and rhythmic, and in addition was truly communal, engaging every man, woman and child in the colony.

There was one more blow in store for the dance, and this came from the attitude of the educators, who in setting up a formula in the Middle Ages for the intellectual training of men (women were not educated), considered the dance neither necessary nor nice. In this they took their lead from ecclesiastic opinion and made certain that the educated man should look upon dancing as a frivolity of kings, a crude pastime of the peasants, or as a questionable entertainment in the theater, usually surrounded by sin. After several hundred years there came a reluctant admission from some that young ladies might have a limited education, and this might include dancing which seemed to be an aid to grace, a quality much admired in the female, even by educators. Romanticism had come in, the female was looked upon as an ethereal creature of grace and beauty, and the emasculated dance, which enhanced these values, was for women and not men. This is the very attitude which prevails today. Although dancing is established as a part of education for women in the United States and elsewhere, ninety-eight per cent of the males are taught only to shuffle around a ballroom with their feet. Every sizable woman's college has a department of dance in these days, but directors of men's colleges still think in medieval terms in regard to dance training.

By the nineteenth century the dance and dance drama had

fallen on evil days indeed. Except for some technical advances in the theater it was far inferior to music, poetry and drama, had lost its dignity, had no cultural purpose except to amuse. The immense impact of opinion, both religious and secular, seemed to be about to smother the original art. The collective attitude was that dance was an inferior activity, at best an amusement, at worst a sin. There were, however, a few artists and philosophers whose lone voices cried out against this loss to culture, whose tongues told where the true values lay. There were not many, and they were widely separated, one of the most eloquent being Jean Georges Noverre who wrote in the middle of the seventeenth century:

> Ballets . . . ought to unite the various parts of the drama, most of the subjects, adapted to the dancer, are devoid of sense, equally unmeaning and unconnected. Dancing . . . ennobled by the expression of sentiment, and under the direction of a man of true genius will, in time, obtain the praises which the enlightened world bestows on poetry and painting, and become entitled to the rewards with which the latter are daily honored.

It was not until the twentieth century that Noverre's prophecy even began to be realized.

Just as the dance was about to expire with a giggle in its tinsel dress, a marvelous flow of dance genius came in such an abundant stream that this tattered and beaten sister of the arts came to life with the glow and vigor of a young Diana. The opening years of the twentieth century saw the Russian Ballet startle the world with its matchless dramas, dancers and choreographers. In quick succession there appeared Isadora Duncan, Ruth St. Denis, Mary Wigman, to mention only the peaks of genius, and finally the modern American dancers, Martha Graham, Hanya Holm, Charles Weidman and others.

Now in the middle of the century, some progress has been made to restore the dance drama to a significant place in our culture, but probably it will be long, if ever, before we match again the great period of the dance drama, the apogee, when each man, woman and child took part in great dramatic festivals with heart, soul and body. Even the savage, so contemptuously regarded as uncivilized, knew a greater, because more deeply felt, dance theater than we are ever likely to know. The modern theater, movie house, gymnasium and studio are only partial substitutes for these former great experiences, but they are the best we have for restoring some of our lost oneness, and even this is perceived as yet by only a few.

The contention of these few is that dance, and dance drama, persistently robust after thousands of years of snubbing by asceticism, scholasticism and puritanism, can make profound revelations of that which is significant in the relations of human beings, can restore the dignity of the body, which prurience and hypocrisy have damaged, can recall the lost joys of people moving together rhythmically for high purposes, can immeasurably improve the education of the young, can, to a much larger extent than it does, restore vitality to the theater, can contribute a moral stimulus to the furtherance of more courageous, coordinated and cultured behavior.

And this dance will have nothing in it of the inane coquetry of the ballet, or the sensual convulsion of the Negro. It will be clean. I see America dancing, standing with one foot poised on the highest point of the Rockies, her two hands stretched out from the Atlantic to the Pacific, her fine head tossed to the sky, her forehead shining with a Crown of a million stars.   —ISADORA DUNCAN

I am certain that movement never lies . . . I am not saying that a good person makes a good dancer or that a bad person makes a bad dancer. The motivation, the cause of the movement, establishes a center of gravity. This center of gravity induces the co-ordination that is body-spirit, and this spirit-of-body is the state of innocence that is the secret of the absolute dancer.

—MARTHA GRAHAM

WALTER SORELL

Two Rebels, Two Giants: ISADORA AND MARTHA

THE GREAT creative artist who breaks away from the traditional concepts of his time and tries to find a new way of expression is no accidental phenomenon. There we see him walk far ahead of us, off the beaten track, unique in his appearance, in this underlined dramatic otherness of his, willful and capricious—and yet, in spite of such apparent isolation and self-imposed solitude, he remains part of the total, akin to the pulse-beat of his time. But an urge so great that it seems inescapable

Martha Graham, "rebel and giant" of the modern dance, in *Acrobats of God*, a humorous danced paean to the world of the artist. Set by Isamu Noguchi

Photo by Oleaga; courtesy of Martha Graham Company

forces him to break out of the cobweb of conventional ideas and forms; and because of this desire, however inexplicable even to himself, his vision is able to carry him beyond the lines demarcated by his contemporaries.

This urge to seek new ways of expression is conditioned by cause and effect, by action and reaction in the development of society. It seems that whenever a cultural phase reaches its peak of saturation, it creates in itself the spirit of its own antagonist. Thus, at a certain point of history, the revolutionary artist anticipates a new form and content of life which, at that time, has become ripe for him as he has for his time.

No time has ever been more ready for decisive changes than that of the turn of the century. When we speak of the "gay nineties" we visualize women with wasplike waists sweeping the city streets with their froufrou ruffles; women on bicycles and men with monocles; the air filled with the effervescence of champagne and the echo of cancans from dancing halls; overstuffed rooms with bric-a-brac from the orient which the white man was just about to divide and exploit; everything was "fin de siècle," and one recited poetry in cozy Turkish corners with the divan half-hidden behind a bead portiere. But behind all this sham glitter and laughter was an uneasiness and weariness and a meaningful "after-us-the-deluge" attitude. One was not sure of whether it was the end or a new beginning. One began to see that not all was well. Ibsen's Nora had just then slammed the door of her doll's house behind her. The machines caused unrest, strikes. One was frightened by Hauptmann's *Weavers* and shocked by Zola's *Nana* and *Germinal*. One could not help reading Oscar Wilde, Dostoievsky and Tolstoi, and about man's growing awareness of his responsibility toward man. In short, one was frightened, and cushioned one's fear with plush.

On the other hand, the turn of the century, to be more exact the decade between 1895 and 1905, clearly shows the revolutionary trend in man's feeling and thinking as an antidote to his "all-out escapism." His dissatisfaction with the old concepts of the world he lived in led to a fervent groping for new form and content in all spheres of activities. The revolutionary changes were, so to speak, in the air.

Materialistic science received its death blow. Madame Curie, Professor Roentgen, Koch and Pasteur kept the world breathless at the time when Edison electrified it; Freud began to probe the underlying sources of our way of being; Einstein dented the old basic concepts of physics, Schoenberg questioned the bases of the tonal system, and, somewhat later, Picasso tried to reduce figures and objects to their fundamental geometric forms and to turn the abstraction of these forms into new artistic designs.

Only when we recall that time to our mind, that condition of man's mental and physical state, can we understand the new era of dance which began with Isadora Duncan. In retrospect, her daring and deed appears, first and last, as the utter negation of her time. The affirmation came later, actually came after her. She was not the irresistible performer whose technical form of expression would still be remembered many generations later. No, she was the torchbearer of a new idea, the rebel who laid the groundwork for the dance of the twentieth century.

When Isadora "rediscovered" the dance, the Russian ballet was chained and paralyzed by an autocratic bureaucracy and its artistic output was tagged "Mental Stagnation." It had then become stereotyped in the expression of form and idea, or, as Lincoln Kirstein said, it had "petrified into a formula for technical display."

Isadora rediscovered the dance through the discovery of her body. She worshipped nature and her first dance masters were "wind and wave and the winged flight of bird and bee." She felt the immediateness of nature expressed in her own body and was out to evolve her "movements from the movement of nature." How can any body function when it is not free from the constriction of whalebones, the stuffiness of the tulle ruffles and the gaudiness of jewels? The nude is the noblest in art, she cried out. The right conception of beauty can only be "gained from the form and symmetry of the human body." And what is dance if not beauty awakened in the human body? And from there one step further: body and soul must grow so "harmoniously together that the natural language of that soul will have become the movement of the body."

First came her negation of the then dominant type of ballerina with the frozen coquettish smile, the negation of decadence and imitation of bygone times, the negation of meaningless, machinelike movements, of outdated acrobatics. Then came her enthusiasm for the Greeks which was her detour to find her way back to natural body expression. When she used the Hellenic freedom of the body, she was looking for some kind of prop, and for an incontestable ally in her fight for her ideals and for recognition.

What she danced was not really what the ancient Greeks might once have danced. She realized it herself when she said that her dance was American, that it was born of the woods and the sea and the eternal spring of California. But she maintained that to find the dance again as free movement and as creative force, one must go as far back as the Greeks in history and the instinctive movement of child and animal in life. Because they, and they alone, move according to their form and frame, their organic structure—not artificial, not construed and contrived, not angular.

Angularity was the one thing she could not perceive at all and which she detested most. And here again she proved to be of her time, imbued with the neo-romantic spirit of those days no matter how far ahead of her contemporaries she actually was. She saw no angular movement in nature, no full stop put behind any movement to denote its end. There were only undulating lines which never came to any stop.

Her art was lyrical and, as such, highly personal. She believed in "the divine spirit through the medium of the body's movement." She believed that "spiritual expression must flow into the channels of the body, filling it with vibrating light." But where can it come from if not from the "soul"? For her, all emotional experiences were the origin and seat of expressive movements. We must not forget the time had then come to make man stop and probe his self.

That was what Isadora Duncan did in her own way. She probed her self. She may have meditated in front of a mirror (and did she not stand before an imaginary mirror her entire life?), seeking the physical release for all that went on in her spiritually. She waited for the moment of emotional stimulation to find the right expressive movement for what she felt. The stimulation had to come mostly from outside, from music. But she did not interpret it. Its function was to make her creative impulse function. What she interpreted was nothing else but her inner feeling, her unconscious stream of thoughts, her tumultuous physical desires. Such expression could hardly be stimulated by the then prevailing custom of dancing to cheap Italian tunes. She did away with them and turned to serious music: to Gluck (who was her favorite), Wagner, Beethoven, Chopin. It was their music that inspired her "soul" which, in turn, flew "into the channels of the body." As she said in one of her lectures (Berlin, 1903), it was precisely at such an inspired moment that she tried to find the *key movement* which every dance needed and from which the other movements would emanate, like a motor phrase from which the power of movement would evolve its own forms.

But was her main merit to "recover the natural decadences of human movements," to fill and shape them with emotional content? That she gave freedom and content to the expression of her body was but the first step into a new direction. To see what she did from an artistic viewpoint only would limit the scope of her deed which was not merely the deliverance of the dance from the shackles of the past. She aimed at the deliverance of man through the dance. This became clear when she spoke of how astonished an intelligent child must be

> to find that in the ballet school it is taught movements contrary to all those movements which it would make of its own accord. This may seem a question of little importance, a question of differing opinions on the ballet and the new dance. But it is a great question. It is not only a question of true art, it is a question of race, of the development of the female sex to beauty and health, of the return to the original strength and to natural movements of woman's body. It is a question of the development of perfect mothers and the birth of healthy and beautiful children. The dancing school of the future is to develop and to show the ideal form of woman. It will be as it were a museum of the living beauty of the period.

The ideal form of woman as Isadora saw it was not the Gibson Girl of her time. Small wonder that the America at the turn of the century—then in the last phase of her "Gilded Age" and dragged into McKinley's imperialistic adventures—rejected Isadora. The feelings were mutual, and as if into a self-imposed exile she went to Europe where she finally triumphed.

That she shocked the people wherever she went was in the nature of her personality. When she rediscovered the dance through the discovery of her body, undoubtedly sex was at the root of her drive to dance. She always remained the apotheosis of sex, vacillating her entire life between the purest maternal instincts and those of the adventure-seeking woman. Only the dignity which lay in every move she made, in every word she uttered, kept her from slipping into the cheap and profane. And it seems that this most primordial of our instincts was the very source of her strength and greatness.

Whatever she did was a slap in the face of all established norms and codes. She was a rebel who stormed the barricades of law and order, of rule and regulation. It was a time for rebels, and she was one of them. In the utter negation of the past lay the realization of a new era. She opened the door on the threshold of this era, and a new vista became visible, different from what was known before. It matters little that she was unable to really fulfill her creative task. Perhaps her character—the same character which gave her the impetus and strength to rebel—defeated her in the final fulfillment of artistic creation.

When it is true that every century may have its Napoleon, but not every Napoleon his century, Isadora found her time ripe for her. She restored the human body to its natural rights, after man had neglected it for two thousand years. She delivered the dance from the fetters of mere entertainment and recreated the art in its oldest form of expression: the expressional dance. And with the return to the freedom of movement and with the discovery of the awareness of our self, Isadora Duncan anticipated the conception of modern man.

2

Martha Graham dances the modern man: his personality in the abstract, his hopes and failures, his frustrations and inner conflicts, no matter whether she uses American folk material or goes back to Greek mythology.

About the same time Isadora gave her last recital in Paris (and shortly afterwards lost her life), Martha Graham gave her first recital in New York. A mere coincidence? No doubt. And yet it carries symbolic significance.

To set these two great dancers in juxtaposition is an attempt to draw a painting in contrasts, though there are, sociologically seen, threads leading from one to the other.

If Isadora was a beginning, Martha was its fulfillment. In retrospect, it seems that Isadora's method was, as a most personal expression, limited to simple walking, running and leaping. It was soul minus technique, while Martha is technique plus soul. What was still a never-ending groping for new form and content with

Isadora—vague, however impressive it may have been—has found in Martha its master.

Opening her soul; seeking her inner self still with the help of a mirror; turning her feelings inside out in uncontrolled effusion, with her sex somersaulting: that was Isadora. Martha came of age with psychoanalysis; she had the advantage of a whole generation's experience over Isadora; she is sparing in her expressive language to such an extent that she only communicates the essence of her innermost feelings; she is all restraint, complete integration.

In imitating nature, Isadora tried to give the impression of wind and wave and bird; it is true, she no longer escaped the ground as the ballerina did, but she merely made use of it, since it was inescapable. Not Martha; for her the floor is vital, she has used it as an expressive area and has thus added it as a new space to the dancer.

Martha Graham revolutionized the dance vocabulary, and expressional dance as well as ballet have received a durable contribution through her technique. She broke completely with the idea of the flowing movement of the ballet and the lightness which is out to conceal all effort. She also felt that the undulating lines of nature, their rounded-off beauty—in which Isadora still so fervently believed—were a mere photographic repetition if expressed through dancing. Not unlike Picasso, or modern architecture, she tried to find the basic geometric form of the object, or idea, which she wanted to shape, and from there she went one step further to give the abstraction its new artistic form and face.

In revolt against the flowing movement she evolved a new language of symbols and finally arrived at what she termed percussive movements which take hold of the entire body in form of a beat, of contraction and release. She also evolved suspensions and falls from different positions and in a variation of accents and speeds which she applies to the expression of different emotional stages. Her entire body became a most articulate instrument in a fully coordinated manner: legs, shoulders, hips, face and hands welded to an entity which can only be achieved through the highest form of technique. And "technique," Martha Graham said, "only services the body towards complete expressiveness."

After a process of thorough elimination, after trial and error, she always tries to find the rudimentary expression of her inner experience. In its almost epigrammatic conciseness it loses its pictorial effect, becomes angular and, through the newness of its image, remains sometimes as obscure, or not immediately fully comprehensible, as a passage of one of T. S. Eliot's poems.

She was often criticized for appearing intellectual or even cold. It must be said that some of her dances strike us as unfamiliar, but everything ceases to be unfamiliar after a certain time. Her dances have inner passion, since the urgency to create is, with her, always emotional, never the result of mere thought processes.

Only the essential is tolerated, in movement and stage sets. And having reduced everything to the movement necessitated by the inner feeling, she arrives at the intensification of her self. Of her earlier period, it can be said that her approach had much of the American landscape, of purposeful soberness like the American cities—and is just as impressive. It is modern Gothic, made in the u.s.a. Martha said that

> nothing is more revealing than movement. What you are finds expression in what you do. The dance reveals the spirit of the country in which it takes root. No sooner does it fail to do this than the dance begins to lose its indispensable integrity and significance.

More and more, her compositions gain in poetic insight and are driven by an intense feeling. But there is so much awareness in this insight and feeling, such a complete delineation of psychological processes and such a wide range of symbolic images that we can often only grasp their depth and meaning after seeing and re-seeing these compositions many times. It may sometimes seem to lack clarity where, in fact, she has reached an expression that is the most concise presentation of what she has to say.

Lately, her compositions deal with emotionally complex situations and conflicts which can be termed psychological dramas. We can easily see how she delves deeper and deeper into the intricate problems of the inner processes of man: From her *Letter to the World* in which she portrayed the alter ego of Emily Dickinson to *Deaths and Entrances*, the tragedy of frustration, to *Judith* in which she tries to communicate the inner struggle of the woman who feels called upon to rise to the greatness of her deed.

It is this constant probing into what motivates human conduct, her total introspection into character and her characterization with all deeper psychological implications which sets her apart from all other dancers of her time and makes her exert such great influence on them. Martha Graham found the dance image of our "age of anxiety."

3

Isadora may well have been the initiator of the idea of the expressional dance, but her method was so personal that no school could continue where she left off. On the contrary. America's modern dance leads back to a dancer whom John Martin called "the antithesis of Isadora's" nature and art.

With the establishment of the colonial empires at the turn of this century, white man not only profited by the exploitation of the colored races, but the opening up of a new and exotic world also stimulated his imagination. Dreamlands had been found for those who wanted to escape the industrialized pattern of life without necessarily having to part with its comfort.

The oriental influence on literature and the arts in general had never been greater than at that time. Ruth St. Denis became entangled in the rich embroidery of oriental movements. She was not as dramatic as Isadora, she was spectacular. She knew how to give a great show, she reveled in light and color, in costume and scenery. But what gave St. Denis' dance the individual imprint was her ardent belief in mysticism and her desire to transplant the exotic and ritual dances of the Far East to America.

Her art, her lavish theatricalism was one form of escape, it was entertainment and stood in utter contrast to the growing problems of her time. The first quarter of this century was seething with all kinds of "isms" in the arts. The machine had changed the pace of man. Restlessness and riots were everywhere, and the growing awareness of a looming disaster. The First World War whipped the emotions up to a high pitch: the war to end all wars; hope for freedom, and the League of Nations. And then the great contrast of two worlds: Europe, the sea of disillusionment, frustration and fighting ideologies; America, an island of safety, security and wealth. Man lived in an atmosphere of stark realism and materialism. In utter confusion and fear of himself, he looked for relief into *himself*, searched for new self-expression and threw himself into new adventures, politically and artistically.

Martha Graham grew up in this period of growing strife and awareness, with the world's problems and man's predicaments piling up higher and higher. She was the first dancer of the Denishawn group to make herself independent. When she rebelled artistically against the artificiality of Denishawn, she felt forced to seek the adequate expression of what was then going on in her and around her. If "movement never lies," as she said, then she had to find her own language, the idiom and image that would express, in her medium, her own self and the self as reflection of her time. In other words, it was finally impossible for her to continue with the impersonation and representation of Hindu gods and Aztec warriors and oriental stories. Martha turned against the "music visualizations" and the rigidity of alien concepts which were not only alien to the American spirit but also to the problems of her age.

When Isadora Duncan dreamed of the great American dancer who would raise the dance to "the most noble of all arts" again, and when she saw "America dancing, standing with one foot poised on the highest point of the Rockies, her two hands stretched out from the Atlantic to the Pacific, her fine head tossed to the sky, her forehead shining with a Crown of a million stars"— then she must have visualized the image of Martha Graham.

In the instinctive and organic life,
in the mental and spiritual life of man, characteristics make themselves
felt which demand communication. Man turns to man. Man needs
man. Art is communication spoken by man for humanity in a language
raised above the every day happening. What would be the sense of an
art that robs itself of its communication and arrogantly believes that it
can turn away from man? —MARY WIGMAN

HANYA HOLM

The Mary Wigman I Know

ART GROWS out of the basic cause of existence. From there it draws its creative and constructive forces. From there it receives strength to renew, rejuvenate, transform itself. And there only is it imperishable, eternal."

These are Mary Wigman's words. It is her belief that the artist must absorb the primordial elements of life during the process of creation, that he must lose himself in something that is greater than himself, in what she calls "the immediate, indivisible essence of life." Caught by life's majestic current, the artist becomes excited and stimulated to express his experiences. His existence as an individual may be extinguished in the midst of life's current, but he is rewarded for it by the singular gift of his participation in the all-embracing, universal happenings of his time. He readily absorbs the energies flowing into him, but this steady flow of energies will, at various points of culmination, force him to action. These forces discharge themselves in the dancer as move-

Hanya Holm, one of the pioneers of the modern dance, is shown here in one of her solos danced in 1937—before she became a vital force in the field of the lyric theater

ment—as the dynamic and rhythmic visualization of his life experience.

To Mary Wigman the dance is a language with which man is born, the ecstatic manifestation of his existence. It is the entity of expression and function, pellucid corporeality, a form made alive through the pulsebeat of experience. To *know* is not enough; where knowledge can no longer reach, where only the inner emotional experience becomes sole and supreme law, there the dance begins, the dance in which body and soul become an indivisible entity, or "the body, visible manifestation of its being, turns into the truthful mirror of its humanity."

2

Mary Wigman's dance creations emerge out of her awareness of her time and her almost demonic urge to give artistic form to reality, as mirrored within her, and to animate this form with her breath. Although man, arrested in his time, creates his most personal and specific form, it is never an arbitrary form invented by one person for any individual purpose. It develops with the individual, unchecked by any borderlines, reaching beyond oceans. The expression of the dance, its style and content, its intellectual basis and emotional impact, is the symbolic image of its time. And the artistic creation of the individual himself gains importance only through the establishment of a relationship between his ego and mankind.

But does Mary Wigman express mere "feelings"? She would say no. They are not feelings we dance; feelings are already too clearly delineated, too obvious. We dance the constant change of mental conditions, as they are alive in man as a rhythmic flow. The dance content must be like the content of any other artistic medium: its nuclear point must be man and his fate. Yet, not "the fate of man of today, yesterday, or tomorrow," but of man as the immortal phenomenon that arises, grows and dies, that is always the same and, in spite of this sameness, always different. It is not the personal problem, but the universal-human problem which becomes her main motif.

She strongly believes in any great work of art as growing out of a necessity. Every idea has its own inherent law, the rules of which develop during the creative process of each composition. Therefore, it becomes impossible to make them fit any other composition, should they not deteriorate to mere formulas. And formulas strangle the creative spirit.

With her, every creation seems to be a spontaneous, almost volcanic eruption of feelings suddenly freed and turned into visual images. But this suddenness is deception. She said once that "the idea for a dance comes to the creative dancer, so to speak, in his sleep, in other words, suddenly it is here. As a musician hits upon a melody without knowing where it comes from, thus the dancer's movements come spontaneously to his mind." Yet the dancer may have carried the idea around with him for a long time without finding its visual shape. Set into the world by an experience, of which we may or may not be conscious, it is a wearisome process until the foetus-idea grows and develops in our mind only to be set free, to take the form of an independent artistic life after much labor and final discharge through inner friction and tension.

While molding and shaping her inner experience she tries to purify what is most personal by making it impersonal and valid for everyone. What she demands from herself and every artist is the feeling of responsibility for form and content, for the absolute clarity of the visualization of his idea and for the ideal postulate that every genuine composition must be a confession, must bear testimony of the artist's own being and, beyond that, of mankind as reflected in him.

Her creations are unsophisticated. She draws from rich sources of symbolic-primitive origin. Although her dance compositions show a strong leaning toward mysticism, they are never cryptic; they may be "heavy" with symbolic meaning, but never get out of hand nor lose themselves in obscurity. Here her intellect works as a moderating, controlling factor. It elevates her topics to a level of universal importance.

In her *Witches Dance* (1926), for instance, it was not her idea of visualizing broomstick or Walpurgis Night, but the deep-bedded darkness in man, the wicked and witch-like trends in the human character. In this dance as well as in her *Ceremonial Figure* and *Dance of Death* she uses masks to underline the symbolic power behind the reality of the dancing figure. In her opinion, it becomes necessary for a dancer to hide his face behind a mask, if the creative spirit forces the performer from a realistic plane into the realm of irrationalism. Masks should never be used as a decorative accessory; they must extinguish the dancer as a person and help transcend the performer into a sphere in which vision and reality become an entity; they can accentuate the struggle of the individual against the forces of the universe as well as his own struggle with himself when part of his ego becomes liberated from his total ego and, in his dualistic fight, the dancer's creation turns into a seemingly alien figure.

What makes Mary Wigman appear so typically "Germanic" is her preoccupation with death and the Faustian in her personality and compositions, two factors which, often misinterpreted, have led to misunderstanding of her intentions and, consequently, to strict rejection of her art.

But it would be erroneous to assume that this rejection, this bewilderment and confusion caused by her dances, was restricted to America alone. From the very beginning of her career, every audience has gone through a shock experience which probably was repeated at every performance she gave. It was created by her so definite attitude to the profound and profoundly human problems she dealt with, by her portraits of the eternal struggle of the self with itself and the environment whose product it is. When she came to America in the beginning of the 1930s, she had already achieved world-wide reputation. But even then the voices of the doubters and deniers were still heard in her own country where it had taken her years of endurance and a strong belief in herself to overcome the opposition of public and critics alike ranging from indifference to loud derision. She says in an autobiographic fragment about these formative years: "Belief, despair, belief in a constantly changing flow of back and forth. And something in the back of my mind that was a 'must' which forced its 'will.' Fatigue and exhaustion were states of transition. Climax and depression have gradually manifested themselves as a rhythm of creativeness conditioning one another. The most difficult was to learn patience and to have to wait without losing one's strength through the years; to experiment without interruption."

After each performance, after each new attempt she would call "herself to a most private trial where she had to account for every movement." And every time the result is the same—a qualified sentence: "Not yet strong enough, to begin once more from the beginning." This is the Faustian in her character: the constant conflict between the aim she strives for and the errors she succumbs to, but never to yield, since Satan dwells in the temptation to be driven like flotsam instead of striving for the higher aims. The Faustian in her work: to overcome man's instinctive cravings, the average man in us; in order to be able to exist, one has to place oneself on a higher plane of awareness, to decide for a constant struggle to secure such awareness and to decide against the peace of doubtful happiness.

Therein lies the thought of "sacrifice" which is uppermost in her mind and finds its way into her compositions time and again. Everything that is, in short, total existence is dependent on and subjected to the idea of sacrifice, knowingly or unknowingly, intentionally or unintentionally. The offer of such sacrifice has a sacerdotal connotation: to sacrifice on the altar of mankind.

In the hourly enacted drama of life and death, in the struggle with life and against death must lie man's readiness to die. In the same way as she pleads for living the day in a Dionysian manner (Dance for the Earth), her many dances on death are by no means distorted, never despairing or accusing. In them is the courage of readiness which may be full of tragic elements, but in a dramatic-heroic sense only. Mary Wigman is so deeply rooted in life that she finds in the symbol of death (which she is so often tempted to express artistically) a counter-balance to her dynamic energies of life. Death is the only point of rest, a pause, an oasis where the soul, forced into a welter of desires and demands, finds peace. The face of death has nothing frightful about it. Death is not the end, it is a suspended state.

3

Consciousness of her time and the strong link with which she is tied to her fellow-men are shown in her indomitable belief in the group dance.

"It is not the soloist's achievement which is pregnant with future," she says. "This will always remain a single and purely personal maximum achievement . . . But the young dance generation should put all emphasis on the group dance. There are all possibilities, there is future."

Mary Wigman feels that the development of every dance personality should take place in two different directions: the perfection of the performer as an individuality and, on the other hand, the adjustment of this individuality to a group.

The dancer who choreographs may bring with him a blueprint of his idea. But this, though it may be necessary, is only the smaller part of his work. He must be so convinced of, so overwhelmed by his visualization that his own experience can become the dancer's experience and that finally a single basic chord embraces the entire group. Unlike a conductor whose co-workers play from a printed score, the choreographer works with live material, he has to utilize the creative ability of each instrument and must, in fact, help form this creative ability without destroying the personality of the individual performer within the group.

In the awakening of the group to a communal rhythmic pattern there lies, to some extent, self-denial of individual expression. But this yielding of ground is not lost. It is absorbed, incorporated and brought back to life in the totality of the group's creation.

Mary Wigman as a teacher molds independent creative life, helping other talents to mature and to become an active force in the growth of her group. She watches each individual modulation to find the one forte which every personality has. She aims to transfer mere body into a sensitive dance instrument. This is a matter of patience, endurance and discipline. "Woe to the dancer who loses patience!" she said. "He will never find the way to the essence, to the resources and innermost motive of his dance. He will remain the self-centered Ego-Dancer whose language is masturbation. But never can he become a body of expression of all those things which, beyond his own ego, reaches, embraces and stirs other people."

Mary Wigman recognizes three basic stages in the development of the growing dancer, stages which may differ as to the student's abilities, that is in degree, but, nevertheless, show these common features:

(1) *The unconscious expression of the dancer's creative force*, with its instinctive groping for expression regardless of form or content; the realization of the dancer's body and the chaotic experience of its expressiveness.

(2) *The experience of artistic crystallization*, with a gradual division of expression, content, form and function; the general expression in struggle with the individual expression, lack of unity, vacillation between expression for expression's sake and form for form's sake; the body no longer exists as a body only, but is not yet instrument.

(3) *The conscious expression of the dancer's creative force*, expression and function of body have crystallized and are fusing into an entity; dance develops as a language; the body is no longer

self-willed substance, it becomes a means leading to an end: the bodily instrument and its full use by its master, the dancer.

From here on begins the hard road to artistry. The teacher has completed his work on the raw material. Now the dancer needs more hard work, self-discipline and the teacher's counsel and guidance. "The necessary corrections on the bodily instrument cannot and must not be performed according to any generally valid norm, they must stem from a human and artistic understanding of the individual and his most personal expressiveness." Her aim has never been to educate little Wigmans. Though it is only natural that her pupils grow up in the spiritual and artistic atmosphere which is hers, she sees to it that they can detach themselves from her in time. "If one wants to achieve something," I remember her saying, "one must not have oneself in view, only the work, one must not want success, but achievement. Mistaking the person for the matter, or the person for the idea leads to hidden rocks on which a great many artistic attempts have suffered shipwreck . . ."

4

1919. A war-torn Europe. The conquered people sought to overcome their physical defeat by finding new intellectual values, new forms, new expressions. Out of destruction and uproar, out of the struggle for one's existence, grew the awareness that man was inextricably entangled in political issues which reflected the economic and social revolution of modern man.

It was a time ripe for revolutionary thoughts, for otherness, for the new. Out of this maze of ruin, death and starvation, out of a world of uncertainties came Mary Wigman. She came back to Germany from Switzerland where she had lived and worked with Rudolf Laban. Hardly two decades had passed since Isadora Duncan opened up a new world of ideas, two decades in which civilization had grown rapidly, had developed according to dramatic rules and closed in on its catharsis. Modern man came of age, gave it his imprint with motor and speed on the ground and in the air—gradually leading to total mechanization. The era of a button-pressing world began to dawn. Man began to realize that no ego can exist in a vacuum. The individual discovered himself in relation to his fellow-man and the universe.

Mary Wigman gave it artistic expression through movement. "In the dance, as in other arts, we are concerned with man and his fate . . . the fate of man in the immortal and significant aspects of its endless metamorphoses shapes the ancient and yet ever-new theme of the dance form." In contrast to it, let us quickly remember Isadora's words of "the divine expression of the human spirit through the medium of the body's movements." The two worlds of before and after the first universal conflagration.

What was still lyrical romanticism in Isadora Duncan became in Mary Wigman the dramatic interpretation of the conflicts within the individual and in relation to the influence of the outside world. When man is the eternal and unchanging theme of the dance, then, consequently, these themes are constantly changing with man's conditions and his fate. They are not timeless, they are time-conditioned. Man must find his own language of expression in every epoch.

What was with Isadora Duncan "soul and beauty" became with Mary Wigman the transparency of the individual's psychological manifestations—in the Jungian rather than Freudian sense —with the subtleness of all emotional shadings. When Isadora began to dance at the turn of the century, modern psychology was in its incipient stages. When Mary Wigman toured Germany for the first time in the bitter winter of 1919–20, modern psychology had come of age.

"In the last analysis, nothing more happened than that the dancer rediscovered within himself 'the dancing human being' and confessed his acceptance of this in the dance . . ." Nothing more happened. She wrote in a new language of movements the story of the human being, the story of his life and death. Her vocabulary was full of dynamics which filled the space. Without ecstasy no dance, she said, and gave it ecstasy. Without form no dance, she said, and gave it form.

Decades have passed. Years have passed. I am left with the memory of something monumental, of something that has beginning and end and the oneness of both—like a great spheric circle that knows no end. It is like the oneness of death and life in one of her dances, *Todesruf*, of the one who calls and the one who is called. And Mary Wigman dancing both: Life and Death. And the climactic moment when Death is waiting for Life that approaches him and slowly covers its face. At that moment, Death waiting for Life is already Life itself, the coming Life.

There is so much peace in this thought and so much hope —hope for the life to come, for the new generation which will dance and build their world on the world of the past as Mary Wigman has done. And they will say the inexpressible, which delights and torments them, so clearly in a language of their own, and with every movement and with every gesture they will write their story of man and his fate.

I cannot endure a work, even trans-
ported far into subjective reality, which is not deeply rooted in the
reality of all of us.
—JEAN COCTEAU

———

CHARLES WEIDMAN

Random Remarks

I HAVE ALWAYS BELIEVED that the audience and the performer
are indivisible. Both artist and audience enter the house—
although through different doors—from the same street.
They have both seen the same headlines, left the same world of
reality behind them. And while the artist puts on his make-up,
the audience leaves its everyday disillusionment in the checkroom.

Real art can never be escape from life. In histrionic terms,
illusions are not false impressions nor misconceptions of reality.
The world of illusion which the audience expects from the artist
is, in fact, the world of their real selves, the image of their own
world, the translation of their hopes and fears, their joys and suf-
ferings into the magic of the stage.

The artist must not run away from himself, from his "center
of being." He is the bearer of a message, and it is his responsibility

to tell it—in whatever medium it may be—intelligibly, forcefully and with his utmost artistic ability. He may sometimes fail in the delivery of his message, but he must never fail in his purpose.

It is often said of the modern dance that it is not easily understood, that its silent language of movement is so intricate as to veil its meaning. But since any dance presentation lives only while it is being performed and since it can hardly be preserved for later in files and books, it would utterly fail to accomplish its task or even to justify its existence could it not clearly convey its message. Only poets, musicians, painters or sculptors can dare challenge their contemporaries with their media of art and yield to the judgment of posterity. The dancer can do this as little as can the actor or singer. L'art pour l'art is for him the death sentence expressed by his own feeble attempt to convince his audience.

I have always been impatient with the "art pour l'artist." Clarity and understandability has remained the basis of my dance creations. Their intent, concerned with human values and the experience of our times, must be carried by the fullest emotional impact the artist can muster. Then, with the conception of the idea, the intelligibility of its message and the emotional intensity of presentation, the artist's primordial task is fulfilled and—however his artistic deliverance may be judged—his sincerity cannot be doubted.

Some may say that I am going too far when I desire to make my dance creations as easily understandable as a movie. But this may explain why more and more I have come to believe in the pantomimic dance drama. The word "pantomime" does not mean to me the presentation of a dumb show, as most dictionaries define it, or the mere telling of a story or action without the use of explanatory words. To me it is the transport of an idea into movement, the animation of the feeling behind the idea, an animation in which suddenly all commas and periods, all silent moments of an unwritten play become a reality in movement. Moreover, it may be likened to that emotional sequence of a growing world of images which we may experience when listening to a symphony, full of logical continuity and expressiveness where words might seem feeble and music inadequate.

I may be prejudiced in favor of the pantomimic dance, because I have found that my gift as a dancer is essentially tied up with my dramatic talent as an actor, or—let us better say—as a mime. The modern mime must be a modern dancer, and as such his entire body must be alive. This cannot be acquired by emotional experience, only by hard physical training. It may be best called bodily awareness. In order to test this bodily awareness in one of my dance compositions, I went so far as to exclude the face, i.e., the facial expression, completely from the pantomimic presentation.

Any idea being projected produces its specific movement and gesture pattern which is, in itself, purely abstract. Though, basically, pantomime is not mere storytelling, a story may be, and usually is, achieved by what is done. But to attain such ends, the means must be determined by strict form, since form alone leads to artistry.

In seeking to reach my audience and to convey my message in the easiest understandable manner, I often chose the channels of humor. There are various kinds of humor, but first and foremost it must be said that, whenever a humorous element is required, it can come only from the performer himself and must be projected by him.

In the beginning I employed the most obvious humor, the sadistic type of humor, the effect of which is almost guaranteed with every audience. However, with time, I was continually looking for a broader expression of what I wanted to achieve, and I attempted to abstract the essence of any emotion projected through movement. Here is an example. Instead of being frantic as, let us say, a minstrel would be when a bucket of water is thrown over him, I tried to convey the same idea without impersonating a minstrel and with no bucket of water causing the emotion. This attempt finally crystallized into a dance called *Kinetic Panto-mime*. In this composition I so juggled, reversed and distorted cause and effect, impulse and reaction that a kaleidoscopic effect was created without once resorting to any literary representation.

It has been a long and arduous way from this comedy panto-mime to Thurber's *Fables*. But my basic approach to subject mat-ter, though it has widened and developed, has never changed. Content and form are equally important to my choreographic pantomimes. I have never believed that artistry can be achieved without adhering to the strictest form, nor that the heart of the public can be reached, if the artist is blind to the life that sur-rounds him or tries to shut himself off from it by escaping into mere fantasy and romance. Art demands that we be part of life and merge with it. Art and life are as indivisible an entity as the artist and his audience.

The most difficult character in comedy is the fool and he who plays the part must be no simpleton.

—CERVANTES

The finest satire is the one in which ridicule is combined with so little malice and so much conviction that it forces a laugh even from those it hits. —G. C. LICHTENBERG

———

CLIVE BARNES

Comedy in Dance

BALLET has a sense of humor, but for various reasons it likes to keep fairly quiet about it. The understandable, if despicable, tendency, grounded in history and sanctified by the hard-dying English, and, for that matter, American, Puritan tradition, to rate comedy lower than tragedy runs throughout the Anglo-American theater. Yet this same tendency prevails when considering ballet, an art of nothing if not elevation, even though it does sometimes keep its feet too firmly on the ground. In fairness it must be remembered that at least in recent centuries ballet has always had to fight for its claim to be taken seriously against well-armed, ill-informed opponents anxious to dismiss it as mere frivolity. The effect of such destructive patronage has been to make writers on dance aesthetics defensively shrill in their insistence on ballet's high seriousness. Guiltily, and often justifiably, afraid of being laughed at, they have adroitly underplayed the idea that audiences can laugh with ballet. Then again, it is unfortunate that since the nineteenth century ballet has become an almost exclusively middle-class entertainment, its audiences have a traditional suspicion of humor, frequently intensified by the still surprisingly wide-spread feeling that ballet is highbrow and probably at its all too subtle best when boring. No one now chooses to remember that the first great dancer to appear at London's Sadler's Wells Theatre was almost certainly Joe Grimaldi, and that clowns and ballet dancers have always been brothers under the greasepaint, although for years these two traditions of theatrical dancing were kept far apart.

When one thinks of the social ups and artistics downs of comic dancing, when one remembers how long comedy was thought of as an enemy to ballet as a fine art, and when one considers the built-in insecurity with which thoughtful writers on ballet customarily approach their subject, it is little wonder that comedy in ballet has found no literary sponsors. No one ever seems to have asked himself what is funny in ballet, or why that should be so. Can dancing, to make some kind of a start, be funny in itself or only funny by associations? Obviously you have only to put a greasepaint mustache on a ballerina and let her innocently dance the Aurora *pas de deux*, and you have made a joke subtly different (and far funnier) from drawing a beard on the portrait of Mary, Queen of Scots, in a school text-book. There are other comic approaches, many of them more practical and most of them more common, but can dancing be funny without any such external help? The question is probably one for an anthropologist, for it might be reduced to whether primitive man has any sense of the comic.

In dancing it is usually the shock of the unexpected that is funny—and classical ballet with its closely tied formal con-ventions can lend itself to anarchic humor. But any movement is capable of evoking a relieved laugh, provided that it is un-expected enough and its context is not threatening. The whole question of comic movement depends largely on what consti-

Myra Kinch and *Christopher Lyall* in *Giselle's Revenge,* Miss Kinch's satiric comment on the ballet classic

Photo by John Lindquist; courtesy of Myra Kinch

tutes the unexpected. For example, if you are watching an acrobat you expect him to turn somersaults, so this is no more funny than a bird flying. But if you are watching a perfectly ordinary-looking businessman in his gray flannel suit walking down the street, and *he* suddenly turns a somersault, so long as he then propitiates your fears by walking along as if nothing had happened, the movement will be sublimely funny. Even so the humor is not really connected so much with the movement itself as with the total action—it is actually just a variant on the mustachioed ballerina joke. This is still not any closer to comic movement.

Obviously what we think is funny is partly a question of individual personality, but, at least in the case of movement, it is even more a reflection of our degree of sophistication or knowingness in any given situation. Show a dancer spinning round twice in a *double tour en l'air* to a savage, and I imagine he would laugh. Show the same thing to any Western man who consciously is hardly aware of ballet and he will have enough sophistication to accept it as a ballet step. Now show a man going round and ending with his back to the audience, and you will probably get the same reaction. But finally show the latter step to another Western man who knows just a little more about the conventions of ballet, and he will laugh along with the savage. This is what I mean when I say that the formal conventions of ballet lend themselves to humor, but the range of that humor changes as audiences become more knowing and choreographers become more daring in their serious invention of dance steps. While innovations may please and surprise us, it only rarely surprises us in a totally unexpected way, and if it does we are more likely to be nonplussed than amused. We accept the choreographer's right to show us new and unusual steps, just as we accept the acrobat's right to do somersaults. This is a fortunate thing for the art of ballet as a whole, but it makes comic choreography unusually difficult. Consequently, comic choreography really requires an element of exaggeration in it, partly perhaps as a sign to the audience that it can relax from its normal attitude of sophistication and slip into a different gear, a different state of emotional awareness. It is as if the choreographer were saying to his audience: "Watch out for this one, it's going to make you split your sides laughing!"

Pure dance comedy is one of the rarest things to achieve in ballet, and the best examples I can think of offhand are the first movement of Balanchine's *Bourrée Fantasque* and Jerome Robbins' *Interplay*. Here you find an abstract dance humor that has nothing to do with narrative and very little with situation, although it has something in common with the perfectly non-specific comedy occasionally found in music. However, by far the most common form of comedy ballet is that which places humorous choreography within a dramatic framework and scores, quite legitimately, a fair proportion of its laughs from the comedy situation and characterizations.

It would be a vast and fruitless task to classify comedy ballets as if they were butterflies to be mounted on cards according to their species. It might nevertheless be worth making a rough attempt to categorize a few of the more obvious comic methods to be found in ballet. Perhaps all comedy can be loosely split into that which makes you laugh for the joy of laughing and that which makes you laugh for a purpose. The latter, which at its best is one of the most pertinent forms of social comment, is difficult in ballet or, for that matter, opera. Social comment is normally directed at the contemporary scene, while the lyric theater with its rigid stylization and basic convention of unnaturalness does not lend itself to contemporary themes. In ballet and opera we have to accept the reality of people who apparently go through life either dancing or singing, and, although this does not normally cause any difficulty or even conscious thought, we accept less willingly when they are dressed like our next-door neighbors.

Nevertheless social comment and satire are not impossible, and before the Second World War Kurt Jooss made a few forcefully satiric ballets which at their best were as piercing as almost anything in the expressionist theater of the Thirties. *The Green Table*, a ballet which stamped itself upon a whole generation, and its grotesquely sinister Men in Black, their faces fixed with grinning masks, posturing emptily around a conference table, summed up the spirit of Geneva. In *The Big City*, Jooss used a similarly acid vein of comedy to etch some of the details of his naïve yet effective montage of a capitalist society. Another work finding its origins in the pre-Nazi Germany of the Weimar Republic was the Bertold Brecht/Kurt Weill/George Balanchine danced-operetta *Anna-Anna*, or *The Seven Deadly Sins*. Weill's hurdy-gurdy music also inspired one of the few British dance satires, Antony Tudor's *Judgment of Paris*. This tragicomedy set in a sleazy Paris clip joint is the most hard-hitting comedy in the current dance repertory created during the formative years of British ballet in 1938. Its three pathetically laughable whores trying to entertain their solitary drunken customer are as funny and sad as Weill's broken-down music. Their shuffling routines are given an apathetic hopefulness and a quality of unromantic truth that makes the audience's amusement take on an uneasy edge of horror.

Ballet, even satirical ballet, is not usually so uncomfortable—and this is ballet's loss. Far more typical is Frederick Ashton's *Façade*, cocking a gentle snook at the music hall and social dances of the Twenties. But there is no poison in the jest, which is early *Punch* humor; similarly Jerome Robbins' *The Concert* has the more sophisticated air of the *New Yorker*. This is fantasy-satire of a kind perhaps peculiar to ballet and purports to show the wish-fulfillments of an audience lightly daydreaming during a Chopin recital. It has wit, imagination, minute observation (concert-going behavior is dissected with a loving scalpel), and it is riotously funny. But the comment is never bitter. There is the funny-sad, old joke about the woman who buys an extravagantly impossible hat, only to meet another woman wearing its double. There is a sweet, quite telling, joke about conformity: a woman thinks it's raining and puts up her umbrella. One by one the whole company follows suit, they walk around with puzzled looks of unlocated dismay, until they eventually close their umbrellas and face the sun. Then there is a sick joke: a henpecked husband, with a knife in his hand and a murder in his heart, creeps up to his frighteningly com-placent wife, furiously stabbing her in the back, again and again, but all to no avail. Looking at the knife with speculative dis-appointment he tries hara-kiri, which turns out to be supremely effective, and he leaves the stage clutching his stomach in his death throes. The English choreographer Peter Darrell, in an oddly disquieting ballet called *Chiaroscuro*, carries the sick joke further with a danced anecdote about people happily playing blindman's buff with a little girl who turns out to be blind. Here you can smell the blood of true satire, but it's a false scent.

The essential gentleness of ballet humor is almost ines-capable from its economic circumstances. Ballet is an art which depends for its existence on patrons, either private or public. Consequently its organizers must almost always cater to the Establishment, and one of the things even the most easy-going Establishment will not, cannot, stand for is savagery in its humor. The Diaghilev Ballet during its last period actually obtained its patronage by being avant-garde, yet the people who were paying to be shocked only wanted to be pleasantly shocked by an agreeable morsel of the latest ism. They had no wish to be scourged by wit, and I suspect Diaghilev was shrewd and wily enough to realize this—he rarely pressed his luck too far. Admittedly his company produced Bronislava Nijinska's *Les Biches*, a cleverly amusing commentary on the sleeping habits of the bright young things in the mid-Twenties. Any possible harshness was toned down by the ballet's blandly equivocal nature (the page boy who catches the eye of the hero is danced by a girl, and few in an audience pick up the significance of a situation which is not hinted at in the program), as well as being prettified by Poulenc's *café dansante* music and the pastel shades of Marie Laurençin's attractive scenery and costumes.

Audiences genuinely like ballet to be satirical when it pokes fun at itself. Partly because it has so few outlets for the satiric spirit and also because dancing easily lends itself to parody, ballet often turns upon itself with a cannibal-like ferocity unparalleled in any of the other arts, with the possible exception of poetry. The better specimens of this genre—and there are many, for it has been a fruitful field for choreographers —exist on two planes: making specific parodistic references to other ballets for the benefit of the *cognoscenti*, while having farcical movement or jokes aimed at dancing in general to be appreciated by audiences virtually seeing ballet for the first time. A very good example of this *double entendre* is Frank Staff's suite of dance studies, *Czerniana*, created in 1939 in London and still current in the Ballet Rambert repertory. Here the young Staff cut and thrust at his contemporaries with devastating effect. I doubt whether anyone of any sensitivity could ever watch a Massine symphonic ballet straight-faced again after seeing the portentous, yet thrillingly accurate, idiocy of the episode Staff has called *Trop symphonique*. Even audiences who scarcely know *Les Présages* or *Choreartium* roar with laughter at the cheerfully elaborated pomposity.

A much more familiar and perhaps safer target is the nineteenth-century ballet. In Frederick Ashton's *A Wedding Bouquet*, a marvelous *pièce grise* about a wedding in provincial France before the First World War, and for me probably the funniest ballet of them all, the climax is provided by a delicately hilarious parody of a Petipa *pas de deux*, which seems to sting all the more because Ashton claims Petipa as his ultimate master. A blunter, more burlesque form of parody is provided by Antony Tudor's ever-popular *Gala Performance*. Tudor rings the changes by lampooning, with quite scholarly perception, the French, Italian, and Russian schools of ballet in the nineteenth century, with a more immediately appealing study of ballerina foibles and sidekicks at steadily recognizable balletic conventions.

Although *A Wedding Bouquet* and *Gala Performance*, particularly the latter, are strongly satirical, they are also narrative comedy ballets of a far more direct kind than any I have yet discussed. And in this way they fall within the vast majority of balletic comedies. It is perhaps too simple to say that most comedy ballets are funny for the sake of being funny, because there is a great range of humor possible within a narrative framework. Perhaps, in an attempt to narrow the field at least to manageable proportions, I could call them comedies of behavior, comedies of character, and comedies of situation and place them in a descending order of seriousness. It is essential to remember that any particular ballet may contain all these elements, but also that the basic function of comedy is to make you laugh.

Comedies of behavior, or manners, are for obvious reasons less common in ballet than in the drama. Fokine, most civilized of choreographers, working for neither court nor populace but a comparatively select audience, made a few successful attempts at urbanity. *Carnaval* is heartlessly wise on the subject of love, while *L'Epreuve d'Amour*—created when Fokine was older and poorer—treats love with more good humor and humanity. In this fragile piece of *chinoiserie*, where a poor coolie tricks his rich rivals for the hand of the mandarin's daughter, Fokine's carefully observed choreography closely approaches the elegant wit characteristic of the French theater. In *Le Coq d'Or* he produced a parable about valor, a shade too soft for satire and yet not nearly subtle enough for cultivated comedy. Even so, in *Petrushka*, he probably came closer to the spirit of Chekhovian comedy than anyone else in ballet. (But, at that, it was not very close.)

In many of Massine's ballets, his Goldoni-inspired *Les Femmes du Bonne Humeur*, for example, there is a strong element of the comedy of behavior, yet characters and situation are always more important. Just as some writers fill their books with portraits of themselves seen from the different angles of a multitude of mirrors, so Massine's comedies are stamped indelibly with Massine the dancer. At their best, in works like *The Three-Cornered Hat*, there is a richness of comic character- ization that can hardly be equaled. Here is a three-dimensional grotesquerie, a rounded caricature, picked out in preposterously exaggerated choreography with the bulbous, swelling line of a cartoonist. Yet these are not merely puppets in banana-skin routines; their distortions find a basis in life. Massine invented, among many other things, the *ballet bouffe*, but never patented it. It has had many imitations, but the inspiration has been thinned and the characterization reduced to clichés. Quite a few of these imitations are by Massine himself.

If a bad comedy-ballet is good enough to have recognizable traits at all, they will almost certainly be those of the situation comedy. There the choreography lacks the vitality to create characters, and its sole claim to humor lies in the unlikely con- volutions of its narrative line—and this is an exact equivalent to the flaccid drawing-room comedy or front-parlor farce in which the characters speak in no idiom known to man. The situation comedy pure and simple cannot be valid as ballet, because almost by definition it places the prime emphasis on storytelling rather than dancing. Combined with genuine dance characterization, however, it can be among the most entertain- ing forms in the ballet theater, and it includes such ballets as

John Cranko's *Pineapple Poll*, Jerome Robbins' *Fancy Free*, Ashton's masterpiece *La Fille mal Gardée*, and, for that matter, many of Massine's finest works.

Comedy in modern dance has varied from the droll to the zany, from the bizarre to the conventional. One gentle, ironic humorist has been Charles Weidman, one of the pioneers of modern dance and, defensibly, the first to give it a funny slant. Weidman's mild grotesqueries found a companionable spirit in a dance series he produced based on James Thurber's *Fables for Our Time.*

The younger generation of modern dancers has, not unexpectedly, also produced its own crop of dance humorists. Of these James Waring, is the most wayward and maverick; his humor has something of the irreverent, disassociated irrelevance of such playwrights as Beckett. Yet the most humorous figure in the new American modern dance is undoubtedly Paul Taylor.

Taylor never sets out to be funny; his humor is part of his whole approach to life and dance. *Party-Mix* is a wickedly funny satire of New York party-giving and party-taking. *Piece Period* is much more of a simple funny ballet and gets its laughs from basic comedy premises, in a manner almost quaintly old-fashioned.

Perhaps his most considerable comedy effort has been *From Sea to Shining Sea*, a work that tears apart, with affectionate, playful savagery, all that America holds dear. To have cast the Statue of Liberty in a kind of prima-ballerina role is daring enough, but to have made such a statue indulge in what can only be described as un-American activity is blissfully beyond a joke.

Strangely perhaps, for often modern dance is thought of as a highly serious activity, there is a great deal of modern dance comedy. Martha Graham's *Every Soul is a Circus* I unfortunately never saw, but her later, and brilliantly hilarious, comedy *Acrobats of God* deserves to rank among the wittiest of all dance works.

The humor of *Acrobats* is gently urbane. There is no story, indeed there is hardly any theme. Perhaps there is the lightly, deftly sketched suggestion of a dance company, Miss Graham's "acrobats of God." Into this divine circus are placed two equivocal figures: a man with a whip, ringmaster, balletmaster, gentle sadist, and savage buffoon; and a woman, diffidently regal, troubled, elegant, fussy, and—one guesses—a choreographer.

Yet it is not the situation that provided the humor in *Acrobats*, but the enjoyable madness of the choreography. Here the juxtaposition between the real and the absurd is so intimate that Miss Graham is able to mock the classroom techniques while glorifying them. The dancers may be performing bizarre movements, but they perform so brilliantly that one has no sooner said "How funny!" than one is back saying "How marvelous!"

You cannot have comedy without clowns, and ballet dancers are possibly the truest of Grimaldi's heirs. Acting in ballet is quite different from acting in straight theater and requires a different kind of emphasis, indeed an altogether different kind of technique. The general level of acting in ballet is far lower, so far as it *can* be compared, with that found in the legitimate theater or music hall. Yet the great dance actor, uncommon enough in all conscience, achieves, in my opinion, a degree of identification with his role unknown in any other form of the theater. It is the complete fusion of personality and character with gesture; it represents the Stanislavsky conception of acting taken to its ultimate end. In the present century ballet has produced quite a few good comedians, and a handful deserve immortality. Massine, Marceau (although he might object to being included), perhaps the idiosyncratic Frenchman Jean Babilée, one or two before my time, and Alexander Grant, defensibly the finest dancer British ballet has yet had. To see Grant, his eyes shining with stupidity, an idiot grin cutting into his face, dancing like a ramshackle Mercury in *La Fille mal Gardée* is among the theatrical experiences of our day. To see him wavering on the brink of pathos as his dream of happiness fades, and then to see him at the end of the ballet, upsurging and ridiculously, undeservingly triumphant, with a top hat thrust over his eyes and grasping a red umbrella, is to be made aware once more of the nature of comedy.

*Between the adjective possible and
the adjective impossible the mime has made his choice; he has chosen
the adjective impossible. It is in the impossible that he lives; it is the
impossible he does.* —THÉODORE DE BANVILLE

———

ANGNA ENTERS

The Dance and Pantomime: MIMESIS AND IMAGE

MIMESIS IS that form of theater in which a dramatist-actor delineates characters of his own creation with or without speech. The mime is not an imitator. He enlarges, emphasizes, particularizes, accents, comments upon the character he portrays; he is a dramatist who portrays his characters. Mimesis, or pantomime, is universal and in the classic line because of an elasticity which can incorporate dance or any other theater forms required for the realization of images within the dramatist-performer's vision.

It is as though images, either in the creator's memory or in flashes of vision, acting as catalytic agents in relation to aspects of man's life in the world, suddenly decide to have a being of their own. Then the creator as performer has to release these images to take their own form, using whatever theater and other art forms are necessary to their realization.

In that sense, these images-become-characters are symbols, symbols natural to the reality of performer and audience; characters who are our brothers and sisters in whatever time, place and theme—in the sense, say, that Madame Bovary is a character created by Flaubert. Characters, that is, created to speak for themselves.

For this reason, it is preferable that the mime be the creator and integrator of all the arts essential to the fused crystallization of, and comment implicit in, his image's form: costume, setting, lighting, even music. For costume, whether contemporary, medieval or antique, is part of the image's design, with the other component parts fused into the whole composition. Thus, the costume is sometimes the accent as the key or clue to the mode, manner, theme, form, character. So with setting, lighting, music.

This is, of course, one mime's approach to the presentation of images of men and women in characteristic personal moments of their being in contrapuntal relation to a particular period in time, to crystallize a kind of similarity in human behavior down through the ages:

To give personal form to a general experience.

To make the present visible by using it to telescope what was present in the past. It was necessary to see the past through the present, for we see what has been in terms of our own being in the present.

Thus the past would emerge as present, disclosing the essential continuity of the nature of man. The modes, manners and rhythms were merely masks beneath which were the old familiar universal faces of man and woman.

A mode or manner can be concrete as a stone, which when dropped in the sea of human behavior makes a whirlpool in which is swallowed a whole generation and, in time, a civilization.

Yet there always is a thread in that past. In painting it is "the classic line" which always emerges as "modern." And in modes and manners it is always the human behavior which emerges as contemporary.

Topical telescoping of the past in terms of the present was characteristic of the Greek dramatists when they told the sacred myths in terms of their own time. Very faint was the allegory in their references to the political tyrannies, social foibles and idiocies of their own day.

Using a past period as a mirror one might succeed in seeing— showing—one's own time.*

Thus the mime is concerned not only with characters who are tragic or beautiful or noble or comic or pitiful, but also with the *apparently* trivial. Trivial moments in a human being's life, or *seemingly* trivial aspects of it, are sometimes the most significant of character, education and social period. There are trivial moments in a spinster's life quite as tragic, and not only to her, as an Isolde's death or a Cassandra's doom.

The arts are of life; they are not created in a non-objective vacuum. There are no arts without man, and his images are the touchstones of the art forms through which he communicates his vision of the world.

Despite all the definitions and the credos, what remains as the essence of every composition in any art is the image—the image of a color, a combination of color, form, line and space; the image of a sound, or a combination of sounds with silences and rhythms, the image of a smile—one which opens a world in which character is seen, and, through the character, his world.

Many aspects of life seem to me untouched in the theater or in the novel, because in a sense there are no words which quite convey these glints of a smile or a frown, these nuances of human behavior which are the subtle halftones in the scale of human emotions. My feeling was that mime best expressed those images characteristic of human physical movement and expression in the waking and dream states; those nuances of sensation, manners and mannerisms, languors, intonations of expression—the list is endless— which change their form when crystallised in poetry and drama.

---

* Angna Enters, *Silly Girl*, first part of *A Portrait of Personal Remembrance*, self-illustrated. Copyright 1944 by Angna Enters.

I do not impute superiority to mime. Far from it. I merely maintain that mime is a kind of abstract crystallisation of phases and transitions—before your eyes—of life for which words are merely descriptions, however illuminating.*

The description then of mime must be in its own terms, rather than in those of poetry, drama or prose.

For in this theater of pantomime and dance which I am discussing the mime is always his own dramatist. And he is concerned with those aspects of life which are best communicable through mime.

The first mimes were their own dramatists, and later the first dramatic poets were their own mimes.

Mime is the oldest and youngest form of dramatic expression, and the most generally universal. It lends itself in the theater to every form, even to those arts which are not directly of the theater, like some forms of musical conducting; yet it retains its own form. All human beings are more mimes than dancers, in the way in which they walk and smile and weep and dance; in the way in which they tell stories, imitating themselves or their friends or even imaginary characters in some anecdote.

It is *natural* for man to mime, and dance is part of his miming, as making poems and music and drawings are.

Mime, or pantomime, is not the only best means of theater expression. Mime is only best for that expression for which there are no words, or for which too many words would be required.

Yet though pantomime is the oldest and most universal form of theater communication, less is known about it today by most performers than about any other technical medium of their profession.

One reason for this lack is that there is no formula for

---

* Angna Enters, *First Person Plural*, A Chronicle of Self-Education, self-illustrated. Copyright 1937 by Angna Enters.

the learning of mime as there is for dance forms. The learning
of dance forms is of no aid in performing as a mime.

There is a limit to what the human form is capable of in
physical movement. As the "revolutionary" dance pattern becomes more common, it not only loses its appeal as an unusual
design but it takes on an absurd, dated aspect.

Besides, it takes more than an eccentric style in any form
to make a creative artist. Picasso is not an important figure because some of his many styles may seem extreme. In a creative
work one could take away the seemingly eccentric style—and the
form and meaning would remain. In the pseudo the so-called
original style is actually a mannerism—for the pseudo-artist has
nothing to say and is saying it with the most elaborate obscurity,
shrieking all the while: "Don't you dare question me, because I
am modern!"

Today, the persistent notion that pantomime is exclusively
a matter of gestures and facial expressions meaning certain definite words has grown out of dance's attempt to form an alphabet
of literal physical expressions to be used in addition to dance
techniques. The failure of this union finally has led to the use of
spoken lines—by narrators or dancers—with much high-toned
palaver about "a new art." Actually, it is a hoary theatric device.

Gesture seems to have been first with the Greeks in mime
and pantomime—the general distinction between mime and pantomime here being that in the former words were, at first, used.
But the height of this form—mime—was reached, according to
the Greek and Roman commentators, when spoken language no
longer was used. Dance movement was subordinate in the highest
dramatic forms. The Greek was never a professional dancer in
our sense. His professionals were mimes and used dance movements only when necessary. Sometimes dance predominated; more
often, mime.

The time came when a Greek mime-dancer was expected to
"dance with his eyes." And when we reach Quintilian he grows

eloquent concerning the nuances of which gesture without speech is capable. All of the strangulated restrictions of "abstract" dance in the contemporary sense were unknown. Any movement was permissible, provided the combination of movements and gestures communicated an intellectual and spiritual whole.

The Greeks were not interested in form without content— that is, recognizable subject matter in the representational sense. Greek audiences did not expect a performer to enact "set" dances but to elaborate on them. They expected invention and intellectual comment from the professional performer. And they expected the mime to accent the telling of his myth-image—to be a political and social commentator. When he enacted the sacred or profane myths, the mime had to do so clearly and without obscurity.

Articulateness, however, is not a formula. The "classical" school of acting and dancing probably came into being as a last desperate resort due to inability of actors and dancers—I mean those of the past several centuries—to create or recreate the character and period of each play or ballet. This stylized form of expression, whether in ballet, interpretive "classic" or "modern" dancing, "classical" acting or emotionalized gymnastic gyrations in the "Greek" (or neo-primitive) manner, is always the result of learned arbitrarily formulized expressions instead of movements natural to the human body. The easiest way to avoid creating a composition is to think up a formula to apply to all problems. The obvious stylized line is the easiest line to make in drawing, or in dance.

With the rise of the literary theater, in which actors were supplied lines which required little else than their recitation, pantomime settled into the various forms of the unliterary theater— from the commedia dell'arte down through the circus and vaudeville of our own day. The performers in these unliterary theaters retained and developed the faculty of devising their own theater material, or making contributed material their own, and through it achieving a communication with their audiences.

I mean mimes who created their own character, and form of presentation for that character—such as Debureau, Toto, Grock, the Frattelinis, Rich Hayes, Mr. Joe Jackson, Nervo and Knocks, Yvette Guilbert, the Arnaut Brothers, and of course the inimitable Chaplin.

Delsarte, in France, had tried to free the French theater of its stylized form but had only achieved a formula himself. His formula, adapted to opera, theater and dance, succeeded in all but killing mime as a legitimate form of theater expression.

By the first quarter of the twentieth century, mime, as a theater form, had as its only practitioners clowns, mimics and Chaplin. In the dance, except for certain "symbols" left over from Delsarte, mime was frowned upon as the lowest form of expression. In fact, pantomime was denied any place in the dance's sacred grove; it was a twin devil along with "literature." Is it possible that acceptance by audiences of a mime-theater which came into being in 1924 had something to do with the extraordinary about-face of the "pure" dance into every form of theatricalism plus literature?

Of course, even before 1924 there already had been new evidences of a resurgence of mime as a form. With the advent of the Russian Ballet certain great performers again made mime history. Bolm, Nijinsky, Massine—and, in the theater, Feodor Chaliapin.

For, as in the instance of Chaliapin, there were and are other figures in the theater who used mime together with words or song to delineate character, but for reasons of brevity these notes on mime must be concerned only with those who perform without speech.

The mime, incidentally, does not sink into copying or impersonating, which is mimicry. Mime and mimicry are confused in the public mind, but there is no more resemblance between them than between painting and photography. Chaplin is a mime, but those who imitate him are mimics. A mime does not copy another person's actions but invents characters who have their own life, a life quite apart from their creator.

Lucian brilliantly summarized the ideal toward which the mime can only strive, arduously and endlessly:

> You will find that his is no easy profession, not lightly to be undertaken; requiring as it does the highest standard of culture . . . and involving a knowledge of not only music, but of rhythm and metre . . . the exposition of human character and human passion claims a share of its attention. Nor can it dispense with the painter's and sculptor's arts . . . in its close observance of the harmonious proportions that these teach. But above all Mnemosyne and her daughter Polyhymnia, must be propitiated by an art that would remember all things. The pantomime must know all "that is, that was, that shall be"; nothing must escape his ready memory. Faithfully to represent his subject, adequately to express his own conceptions, to make plain all that might be obscure;—these are the first essentials of the mime.

Unlike the formulized dance there is no key set of movements of life expressions for mime. Acrobatic virtuosity plays no part in its projection. Mime is too flowing and subtle, too personal a medium to be imprisoned in a system. Of all the theater forms, mime is most dependent upon the performer for its form; it is the projection of his image. In that projection there must be, above all, a clear, direct conception of what is to be expressed. There can be no nebulous strivings for decorative effect.

In the theater the outward form is projected out into the visual sight line of the audience. In a sense, it is like an architectural drawing in line perspective, with color accents added. Thus, mime is not a theatrical form in which a series of steps and gestures are combined in a variety of movements to make what is generally called a dance.

Because of its nuances of meaning, mime requires in its projection a progression of many forms, some in movement, some non-movements, silences and pauses, all in timed rhythm similar to poetry or song. Actually, mime is very like poetry and song in its composition and presentation.

Performed by a group it necessarily becomes a stylized skeleton to hold together the dancers. A kind of opera libretto. I do not mean that an opera libretto is not a legitimate device but merely that mime does not reach the height of its possibilities in group performance because pantomime is an individual expression and cannot be taught by a director or choreographer.

Stanislavsky, the director of the Moscow Art Theater, realized this in his efforts to make mimes of his actors. I believe it may be said that he was the most successful of any theater director in this medium. But the test of the players of the Moscow Art Theater would have been their ability to project the characters they were portraying without the use of words—of Chekhov or Pushkin.

How then, if mime cannot be taught, is it to be learned?

It would be possible, to be sure, to work out a syllabus, but its value would be relative. For one thing it would be personal to the mime who evolved it, a method of working personal, that is, to one certain performer and, as a result, probably unsuited to others. Chaplin's mime is personal to him and that is why no one has been able to do what he does. His mime has been plagiarized over and over again, but these plagiarisms have failed because they are copies—copies of the outside of a form personal to an originator. Many actors have worked with and been directed by Chaplin; it hasn't helped them.

For what is good for one artist need not apply to another and may only set him on the wrong road to finding himself. This is not a popular opinion, but it is a fact and awareness of it may be the means of making an individual performer or just an

Study for beginning of a gesture.

impressionable pupil-member of a group. No one can teach another how to think.

Schools, and theories taught in them, are the result of art forms and not vice versa. Schools and theories are devised by those who try to discover what it is that makes a given art expression. But they are traps except when a worker in the arts discovers a form for himself through his own experimentation. And this form, because personal, is not transferable.

The young student with a yearning to crystallize his unformed images goes naturally to a teacher he believes can show him the way. Therein lies his first pitfall. If he falls into the downy pit of following his teacher he will be a good pupil but a lost artist. If he questions or discards or accepts only what he can use he will be a disobedient pupil but he is on his way to individual expression.

In the arts, the real culprits are not those who break the "rules" and ignore the "classifications" but those who make them.

Because of the nature of its form, no individual expression has suffered more from rules and classifications than has the dance in which some teachers and performers-become-teachers have tried to impose formulas as "the" dance. Those teachers and certain pundits have unloosed a murky morass of aesthetic gibberish, clichés in which muscular gyrations are entangled in "symbolism."

No one worker in the arts can create universal symbols. He can only crystallize the experience all men and women are heir to. A performer or artist never lived who by himself created universal symbols, but artists always have *recognized* the symbols, and each one gave the symbols his form, so that in his particular form you can see the universals. The modern art movement of the past hundred years has made ridiculously easy the foisting of much that is incomprehensible. Incomprehensible because too many arcane boys and girls have nothing to say. But one is an artist only if able to express in concrete form the image in his

vision. What is "subjective," "unconscious," "beneath the sur-
face," "symbolical," must be made objective, especially in the
theater. Symbols are the result of the experience of the race.
Symbols are communicable or they are not symbols. And it makes
no difference what devices are used to bolster unintelligible symbols—whether these are "functional" stage sets or masks.

In its use of "symbols," the puppet or mask theater has had
its ups and downs. Its downs because after a time audiences tire
of stylized expressions—the mask's bloodlessness, whether an actual mask is used or not—and long for communication between
living human beings, for *living* image-ideas which are part of their
own experience.

In the ability to do this, mime is supreme.

That dancers, both ballet and "modern," recognize this is
evident in the change that is taking place. In the past twenty
years there has been a complete reversal, especially by the "pure"
dance, in the direction of mime. Even Isadora Duncan, towards
the end of her life, planned to venture into mime, perhaps because she sensed that movement without it could lead only to
a blind alley.

For, even without the simplest mime, dance soon palls. To
say that dance must be "pure" or need not mean anything is
nonsense, for the body itself is a symbol of its own meaning.

Leonardo da Vinci said it with his customary clairvoyance:

> O mathematician, throw light on this error. The spirit has not
> voice, for, where there is voice there is a body, and where there is
> a body there is occupation of space which prevents the eyes from
> seeing things beyond the space, consequently this body of itself
> fills the whole surrounding air, that is by its images.

The approach to mime is just the opposite of formalized
dance because in mime self must be forgotten. Self-expression and
mime are at contrary poles.

Because of this there can be no extraneous movements or

gestures for sake of pattern. There can be no fill-in movements separating the continuity of thought in the composition of the image.

In *First Person Plural* I wrote that "dance is composition in movement." This is equally true of mime, but in mime the movement is often seemingly static, is frequently composed of non-movements.

Mime's image-themes should be projected with reservation and good taste; by good taste I mean the appropriateness of each gesture, expression, movement, of the character being composed in the audience's vision. Reserve indeed is one of the prime requisites of pantomime. Florid expressions of the personal emotions of the performer have no place in mime. Thus where mime is used as an adjunct to a set dance form or style it, too, is best in a stylized form.

While it is partly true that it does not matter how one gets one's effects in the theater, this does not mean that a deficiency in one expression should be bolstered by a pastiche of others, any more than in painting a lack of line or form is remedied by spatterings of color. To illustrate, a background of words should not be necessary to convey a pantomime which, I repeat, in its purest form deals with those expressions for which words are unnecessary. There are exceptions, to be sure, especially when the work is a form created wholly by one artist, but the lapsing of extraneous non-related forms, one upon the other, results in chaos.

Clarity is another requisite in mime. It is easier to pretend depth of meaning by obscure pattern, bolstered with poetics, than to achieve simple statement.

To sum up: The mime does not present himself but his idea-image. For this exposition the mime must use recognizable symbols.

These are performed in measured rhythm called "timing"— a rhythm established between himself as performer and himself as audience. If his composition is interrupted by effort on his part to force meaning on the audience in that black cavern beyond his frame, then his continuity, like a spider's web spanning two points, is broken and he falls into an abyss of confusion.

Therefore physical acrobatics and technical showing-off must be foregone. A too strenuous projection coarsens mime as a medium of expression. Leaps, stretches, whirls or contortions—those automatic standbys of dance—may make momentarily exciting and decorative patterns but, like all decorative arts, their patterns, repeated, soon pall. And then another stunt must be devised. Art is not a stunt.

In the Van Gogh still life "Grapes and Apples" one sees the accents which are that painter's endeavor to find for himself the form of his expression. Because of the violence of his strokes this is clearer in Van Gogh's work than in more subtle painters. The bold pattern is not made for the spectator but is the inevitable result of the artist's search for the realization of his own image. And this too is a difference, in painting, between the academic—no matter how "modern" that academic approach is—and the original, the artist and the stuntist.

The same is true in mime. A theater composition in mime must be recreated for oneself at every performance. The accents must be inherent in this re-creation, and not be merely flash to impress onlookers with difficult stunts. The arts are a communication between human beings. Mime is one of those communications, a magic cord of illumination through which the performer transmits images of our world into the past become present. Mime is of the "classic line"—the classic line which is the true and perfect and variable line of life no matter how it is employed. Like a child learning to walk one must find it for oneself.

There is nothing so necessary for men as dancing ... Without dancing a man can do nothing ... All the ills of mankind, all the tragic misfortunes that fill the history books, the blunders of politicians, the miscarriages of great commanders, all this comes from lack of skill in dancing ... When a man has been guilty of a mistake, either in ordering his own affairs, or in directing those of the State, or in commanding an army, do we not always say: So and so has made a false step in this affair ...?

And can making a false step derive from anything but lack of skill in dancing? —JEAN BAPTISTE MOLIÈRE

———

JOSÉ LIMÓN

The Virile Dance

T HE MALE of the human species has always been a dancer. Whether as a savage or civilized man, whether warrior, monarch, hunter, priest, philosopher or tiller of the soil, the atavistic urge to dance was in him and he gave it full expression. He does so to this day. He will dance to the last apocalyptic hour. He dances because he is neither a vegetable nor a rock but a moving organism, and in movement finds release and expression.

Since dance and gesture were his long before the spoken word, he still has the power to reveal himself more truly in this atavistic language not only as an individual but "en masse." At some periods of his history he has danced sublimely; at others with a glittering elegance; and then again he has danced a sad period of degeneracy, or like a clown or a fool, and his ancient power has fallen into atrophy and decay.

King David danced before the ark of the Covenant. He danced not only as the consecrated Pontiff, as intercessor with God for his people, but as chief of state, as head man of the tribe, as the man most exalted and respected, as the racial paragon.

His dance was solemn and majestic, a dance worthy of a king and a man of God. Its cadence and measure were living symbol and embodiment of man's high function and his noblest aspirations. It spoke of the ineffable mystery of man's one-ness with God, for all his frailties and imperfections. The gestures and patterns must have been those of a man who was a king, who was a priest, who was speaking to God for his people. He must have stood tall, his powerful stride that of a man reverent and joyful, his gestures slow with a magnificent dignity, for they must project to the highest zenith.

This was a ritual of surpassing purity and power and showed the man dancer at his most sublime.

King Louis danced before the court at Versailles. He danced various "roles" in the ballets presented there for the delectation and amusement of the court. But always he danced in pomp and splendor as "le roi soleil," "le grand monarque." He performed for as brilliant and corrupt an assemblage of high-born sycophants and courtesans as ever afflicted and disgraced a nation.

The great Louis, like the biblical David, was dancing his epoch and his aspirations. The Sun-King, between bloody and disastrous wars, would while away his ennui with these august spectacles. The wretched and impoverished who were made to die for his aggrandizement and to pay for his magnificence had no part in the festivities. Louis did not in his dance address himself to heaven and pray for enlightenment and guidance so that his people might be blessed and prosper. He was no intermediary, no interpreter, no dispenser of a divine and just omnipotence. These functions were left in the hands of cardinals and archbishops, and they knew their work well.

No, this was another sort of ritual. To an exquisitely formalized code of gestures and steps, the most elaborate of stylizations, dressed in the most glittering and extravagantly beautiful costumes the western world has ever seen, Louis danced this regal debauch. This arrogant, mincing, graceful figure embodied all the perfumed, cynical licentiousness of the regime. Man's highest aim was self-indulgence; the only sin was boredom; the only crime inelegance. This performance was intended to dazzle, to charm, to captivate. This was infamy executed with the flawless delicacy of a "pas de bourrée."

And a recently abdicated king danced like a clown or a buffoon until the small hours of the morning in the fetid cabarets of Paris, London and New York. And this king was not a high priest in mystic communion with heaven, nor a great leader of his tribe, nor was he a magnificent depredator, nor a brilliant luminary in the annals of iniquity.

He was a man dying from boredom, from the terrible spiritual fatigue of his time. And his dance was a ritual of futility and disbelief and unbelief. He had very little. Even the gestures and steps and patterns of his dance were not his own. They had been borrowed (for he was too tired inside to create any) from Africa. But "on him they didn't look good." As he glided and bounced and wiggled he represented the fearful spectacle of a sick world "in extremis." For a moribund society had immolated itself in a catastrophic World War I and, exhausted and spent, was gathering its forces for World War II. The little king and his anemic caricature of the primitive mating dances was symbolic of hopeless fear and despair. Yet in this Saturnalia the frenzy was hollow, the abandon synthetic. It was a dance of a man ripe for extinction, a degraded and unheroic pyrrhic dance.

The modern male as a whole has forgotten the majestic, solemn dance of King David, or the great tragic rhythms of the Greeks, and has accepted as his sole dance experience the diluted trivialities of the dance hall. Or, in the performing arts, he functions, often brilliantly, as an entertainer.

After the Sun-King the dance became more an entertainment and less a ritual. The progressive feminization of its technique, with its emphasis on coquetry and blandishment, were designed to display the charms of a ballerina. The male became superfluous. Those few men who participated were, in effect and function, effeminate adjuncts and supports of the dazzling ballerina. Later these men emerged as creatures of exquisite romantic fancy, as fauns, or the perfume of an exhausted rose, or harlequins.

It was natural that with the general surge of feminism, the female should become the dominant and creative factor in the dance, just as she has fallen heir to the wealth and power of this nation. In the environment of the serious dance the female has won indisputable stature and pre-eminence. Due to the economic factor, the male dancer tends to gravitate to more lucrative aspects of the dance, in musical comedies and the films, which certainly do not encourage serious creative efforts.

There are few men who are content to devote their time to the serious dance and to make their contribution to the regeneration of it as a virile preoccupation. It may well be that the great ritual male dance of our age is the one for which we have been in rehearsal during the last three decades and will presently culminate in an apocalyptic performance, a mighty and appalling choreography across the firmaments, a true Finale, with Viros rampant in jet-propelled, super-sonic chariots, inextricably bound to the fatal rhythm of his era. Truly a pyrrhic dance.

It is precisely because the danger of extinction is imminent that men of caliber and dedication are needed to affirm man's sanity and dance it. No other art offers such a challenge. In a society desperately in need of all its art and artists, the art of the dance offers a rare opportunity for those with the vision of its ancient grandeur to speak of it anew. The few dedicated males should take courage when they reflect that they are perhaps pointing the way. It may well be that we will be a saner world when the President of the United States, as chief magistrate, will lead the nation in solemn dance on great occasions before the dome of the Capitol.

THE DANCE IN THE MAKING

> The true, the unique, the eternal
> subject of a ballet is dancing.　　　　—THÉOPHILE GAUTIER

———

FREDERICK ASHTON

Notes on Choreography

WITH EVERY NEW BALLET that I produce I seek to empty myself of some plastic obsession and every ballet I do is, for me, the solving of a balletic problem.

But let me begin by explaining what I understand the function of the choreographer to be. First of all, he is to the ballet what a playwright is to a play; but whereas the playwright writes his play and generally hands it on to a producer who animates it for him and puts it on the stage, a choreographer does all this himself. Usually he is his own librettist also, so that in a sense the whole fount of the creation comes from him.

When I was younger I created ballets freely, spontaneously and without much thought; the steps just flowed out of me and if they had any shape or form at all, generally it was because the music already had it, and not because I had consciously placed it there. Also, as befits the young, I wanted very much to please my audience and I thought it of great importance that I should entertain, amuse and charm them. Now I don't think that way. Up to a point I don't care what the audience thinks, I work purely and selfishly for myself and only do ballets which please me and which I feel will both develop me as an artist and extend the idiom of the dance.

There are many different sources from which a ballet may spring to life. One can be affected by the paintings of a great master and wish to animate them; one may read a story which

calls to be brought to life in movement; or one can hear a piece
of music which somehow dances itself. And one can have strange
ideas of one's own, or a theme may be suggested by some outside
influence. In the course of my career I have responded to all these
different forms of impetus.

As I said, one can be moved by the paintings of a great master and wish to animate them. This I have done in two or three
of my own ballets, such as my very first which was *Leda and the
Swan*. In this I was stirred by the paintings of Botticelli; I copied
the postures and generally created, I think, the fresh springlike
morning of the world atmosphere of his paintings. I think this
is a very good way for young choreographers to begin. Now that
I am older I rather despise this form of creation, but it is certainly
an absorbing way of working, for it necessitates the study of a
whole period of painting and of manners, and this gives plastic
richness and diversity to the pattern of the dance.

In my ballet *The Wise and Foolish Virgins*, which was arranged to the music of Bach, I went to eighteenth-century baroque but whereas previously in *Leda and the Swan* I had studied
the paintings, in this ballet I not only studied baroque painting
in general but also sculpture and architecture, and I tried to convey, with the bodies of the dancers, the swirling, rich, elaborate
contortions of the baroque period. In this ballet no lines were
spiral, everything was curved and interlacing, and the line of the
dancers was broken and tormented, so to speak. That was a fascinating exercise for me.

As in the two ballets I have just described I studied the visual arts of painting, sculpture and architecture, I would like now
to tell you of another ballet I did, which was taken from a literary
theme. This was called *The Quest*, and came out of the first book
of Spenser's *Faerie Queen*, about the legend of Saint George,
Una and the Dragon. It was an enormous canvas and I must say
that I found it a struggle to give any idea in the ballet of the richness of Spenser's imagery, and quite frankly I don't think I really

succeeded. The danger, in this kind of ballet, is that one comes upon situations which are purely literary and unballetic and are thus impossible to convey clearly to an audience without the use of words; for I personally do not like a ballet in which the audience has to spend three-quarters of the time with their noses in the program to try and find out what is happening on the stage. And I found it difficult, with allegorical characters, to convey clearly their humanity and to bring them to life on the stage as Spenser has brought them to life in his great poem. I personally am not fond of the literary ballet, because it seems to me that there comes a hiatus always in which one longs for the spoken word to clarify the subject. And these ballets seem to lead always more to miming than to dancing, thereby invading the functions of the drama or the cinema. In my balletic ideology it is the dancing which must be the foremost factor, for ballet is an expression of emotions and ideas through dancing, and not through words or too much gesture, though naturally these can play their part. But I am against the overlapping of one into the other, except in the case of intentional music dramas, when all the arts are welded into a whole.

This brings me to my third heading, which is taking one's lead directly from the music, and this is the method which I now prefer. Through it one gets the purity of the dance expressing nothing but itself, and thereby expressing a thousand degrees and facets of emotion, and the mystery of poetry of movement; leaving the audience to respond at will and to bring their own poetic reactions to the work before them. Just as the greatest music has no program, so I really believe the greatest ballets are the same, or at any rate have the merest thread of an idea which can be ignored, and on which the choreographer may weave his imagination for the combination of steps and patterns.

I consider that my own most successful ballets come under this category. The first ballet that I tried in this style was *Les Rendezvous* to the music of Auber. To this gay and sparkling music,

and to the merest thread of an idea—it consists only of young people meeting and parting and meeting again—I wove, I think, a
rich pattern of dancing which worked up to a climax, as did the
music itself. And consciously, all through my career, I have been
working to make the ballet independent of literary and pictorial
motives, and to make it draw from the rich fount of classical ballet; for, to my way of thinking, all ballets that are not based on
the classical ballet and do not create new dancing patterns and
steps within its idiom, are, as it were, only tributaries of the main
stream.

Please don't misunderstand me and think that, by saying
this, I mean there are not great ballets which are literary and pictorial. What I do mean to say is that they are isolated examples,
and that if this line is pursued too strongly it will bring about the
decadence of the dance. If the ballet is to survive, it must survive
through its dancing qualities, just as drama must survive through
the richness of the spoken word. In a Shakespearean play it is the
richness of the language and the poetry that are paramount; the
story is unimportant. And it is the same with all the greatest music,
and dancing and ballets. In a ballet it is the dance that *must* be
paramount.

The great artist is he who in his individual emotions and experiences reflects the emotions and experiences of all mankind, and so by sympathy and knowledge penetrates more deeply into the hearts and lives of his fellowmen . . . So art may be defined in its result as the adequate translation of emotional experience into some external form. It is the expression of the feeling within by means of line, or color, or sound, or movement so that others may share the feeling. —MARGARET H'DOUBLER

———

GEORGE BALANCHINE

Marginal Notes on the Dance

TECHNIQUE is the method or the details of procedure essential to expertness of execution in any art, says Webster. When people, even professionals, speak of dancers as good or bad technicians, they usually refer to their speed or force or physical strength. Technique of the dancer consists of the combined elements of acquired muscle strength and their complete control and coordination. Basically, it is not a question of being able to move according to one's own will, but to move where and how the dancer may be directed.

Only well-trained muscles can execute soft and controlled movements, or any arbitrary movements they are asked to perform. I remember having once watched a strong bird picking up a few thin threads. I was greatly impressed by its arrested muscle strength and the graceful ease with which its entire body moved

Richard Gain and Lisa Bradley in *Sea Shadow*, choreographed by *Gerald Arpino* — the major choreographer for the Robert Joffrey Ballet Company

Photo by Arnold Eagle; courtesy of Isadora Bennett

Erik Bruhn and Lone Isaksen in *Stuart Hodes'* ballet *L'Abbys*, a good example for the constant merging of classical ballet and the modern dance idiom. A production of the Harkness Ballet

Courtesy of Harkness Ballet

towards the little thread on the ground, how its entire system seemed concentrated on that one spot. I felt that its beak could have torn my arm to pieces, so much power was in it; but now it moved with surprising lightness in the direction of its object, with perfect control and coordination.

As in every other art, there are degrees of mastership. Most dancers think they have achieved the peak of their technique when they feel comfortable in the execution of their movements. It is too often, however, a state of "not wishing to be disturbed." They are using the same phrases over and over again and gradually begin to lose the power to progress. But there is another stage of comfort in which the dancer has acquired so much ability that he has no longer to think of his technique, it has become second nature to him. As any good instrumentalist—and no musician can fool his audience as easily as can a dancer—must be aware of precisely this artistic level as a steppingstone to perfection, so must a dancer, in order to be "great," realize that this stage of comfort is the foundation of his potentialities.

Technical perfection must be no more than a means to a desired end: the perfect artistic accomplishment.

I have gradually learned that movements and gestures, like tones in music and shades in painting, have certain family relations and, as groups, have their own laws. The more conscious an artist is, the more he comes to understand these laws and to respond to them. I have tried to develop my choreography inside the framework that such relations suggest.

To achieve unity one must avoid separating elements similar in blood and essence. In spite of the fact that movements may have different names, they may nevertheless belong with each other because of their inner relationship. Only one's artistic feeling and experience can decide on their similarity.

I have often likened head, trunk and arms to a painting suspended in the air. Looking at a painting, we first observe the architecture of its design and the shading of its colors; in most cases, it is the subject matter that strikes us last, also least. We are little interested in who the people are in Rembrandt's *Night Guard*, for instance, or what they are doing. It is the structure of the painting, the almost mysterious distribution of light and shade, the singularity of the half-dark that holds us spellbound, not the subject itself nor the portrayed men; it is Rembrandt's genius behind it.

One is born to be a great dancer. No teacher can work miracles, nor will years of training make a good dancer of an untalented pupil. One may be able to acquire a certain technical facility, but no one can ever "acquire an exceptional talent." I have never prided myself on having an unusually gifted pupil. A Pavlova is no one's pupil but God's.

The ballet is theater, and theater is the magic of a world of illusions. As long as the sweat of classwork is evident on the stage, illusion is defeated. Acrobats can defy gravity and conquer the air. If they aim to create a feeling of illusion, it is of a different nature from that of the dancer. Their intention is to prove complete mastery of their own body; to challenge themselves and the imagination of their audience; and to perform with "ease" in the face of danger. The dancer too must show his mastery of muscular coordination. But he does not stress "ease" in relation to the encountered danger. His presentation is an aesthetic manifestation. The element of danger is, in his case, non-existent, or reduced to a minimum. The acrobat's precision is mainly derived from the necessity of concentration on the element of danger. It lends his presentation the breath-taking quality it usually has. To muster the same concentration, the dancer must imagine that every movement he does is performed on a rope without a net.

In the dance, any leap must have its justification within the framework of the dance composition, otherwise it is pointless. It must produce the illusion of having grown out of the music and the preceding step, in other words it must be motivated. It should never be a piece of showmanship only to prove the dancer's muscular strength and technical skill. This is the acrobat's domain. Of course the dancer must convey the impression that gravity can be overcome by simply lifting himself up and floating through the air. However, since his is not an act but the creation of artistry, his stress cannot be on how to go up into the air, but how to produce the illusion of suspension in the air and how to come down. Landing on the ground again must be both artistically perfect and logical as a prelude or link to the very next step.

We move in spherical ways. Everything that is part of the universe seems to be round. Angular movements, to me, only exist to point out roundness. To speak of angular in a derogatory way is like calling music dissonant. After all, dissonance makes us aware of consonance; so do angular movements make us aware of pleasing roundness. We cannot have the cool shadow without light.

I even see a certain softness and roundness in the straight lines and angular forms of a cubistic painting. We must beware of expressing personal limitations, because all this is a matter of conditioning. When you hear music overamplified for some time, it loses the quality of loudness for your ears.

The same holds good for grace, certainly the most misused noun applied to the dance. No ungraceful movement per se exists, because the most "ungraceful" position can be performed most gracefully. Grace in movement is the final result of one's technical achievement; it is the ability to produce a maximum of dance action with a minimum of effort; it is a climax of consistency and the utter control of balance.

Nor do I approve of the epithet "ugly" in reference to any creation of art. (Only pseudo-art, amateurish creations, can be called ugly.) Mozart was being reproached for having used "wrong" notes in his *C Major Quartet* which one of his noble patrons tore to pieces because of its radical dissonances. What was termed "ugly" more than one hundred and fifty years ago is delighting our senses today. This only proves that absolute truth in art does not exist and that we are being conditioned to accept it unconditionally.

I am so often told that my choreographic creations are "abstract." Does abstract mean that there is no story, no literary image, at best a general idea which remains untranslated in terms of reality? Does it mean the presentation of sound and movement, of unrelated conceptions and symbols in a disembodied state?

I said on another occasion * that no piece of music, no dance can in itself be abstract. You hear a physical sound, humanly organized, performed by people, or you see moving before you dancers of flesh and blood in a living relation to each other. What you hear and see is completely real. But the after-image that remains with the observer may have for him the quality of an abstraction. Music, through the force of its invention, leaves strong after-images. I myself think of Stravinsky's *Apollon*, for instance, as white music, in places as white-on-white as in the passage from the pas d'action appearing on page 99.

For me whiteness is something positive (it has in itself an essence) and is, at the same time, abstract. Such a quality exerts great power over me when I am creating a dance; it is the music's final communication and fixes the pitch that determines my own invention.

Some choreographers seem to be so uncertain of their own medium that not only do they seek the ballet that "has a story" but they also have the story told in words. To me these are no longer ballets, they are choreographic plays. Any amplification necessary must come from the music which may, at times, make use of a chorus. Much can be said in movement that cannot be

* "The Dance Element in Stravinsky's Music," *Dance Index*, Vol. VI, Nos. 10, 11, 12, 1947.

expressed by words. Movement must be self-explanatory. If it isn't, it has failed.

The dance has its own means of telling a story and need not invade the field of the drama or the cinema. The quality of the movement and the choreographic idea decide whether the story is understandable. In most cases, the criterion of success or failure lies in the choice of the subject matter.

Music is often adjectived as being too abstract. This is a vague and dangerous use of words and as unclear to me as when my ballets are described that way. Neither a symphony nor a fugue nor a sonata ever strikes me as being abstract. It is very real to me, very concrete, though "storyless." But storyless is not abstract. Two dancers on the stage are enough material for a story; for me, they are already a story in themselves.

I approach a group of dancers on the stage like a sculptor who breathes life into his material, who gives it form and expression. I can feel them like clay in my hands. The minute I see them, I become excited and stimulated to move them. I do not feel I have to prepare myself. All I know is the music with which I am at least as intimately acquainted as a conductor of a symphony with his score. Of course, the contours of an outline, though sometimes only vaguely, exist in my mind—certain visualizations from listening to the score.

I am therefore greatly dependent on the rehearsal time at my disposal. When Tchaikovsky was once asked how he was able to compose whenever he had to, he is said to have answered: "My Muse comes to me when I tell her to come." Paraphrasing this answer of his, I often say that my Muse must come to me on "union" time.

My imagination is guided by the human material, by the dancers' personalities. I see the basic elements of the dance in its aesthetic manifestations, that is, in the beauty of movement, in the unfolding of rhythmical patterns, and not in their possible meaning or interpretation; I am less interested in the portrait of any real character than in the choreographic idea behind the dance action. Thus the importance of the story itself becomes reduced to being the frame for the picture I want to paint.

In the "storyless" ballet, the question of the costumes and sets gains importance. The stage designer has little to go by if he cannot derive his inspiration from the musical score, as the choreographer does. Then he must be present at the rehearsals and have the choreography furnish him with sufficient ideas. The "storyless" ballet is a great challenge to the designer's imagination, since he lacks any literary stimulation. On the other hand, there are the costumes and sets which can underline and help—with their composition of color and form—to make the visualization of music plastic and dramatic.

The designer must always be aware that the image he produces is part of the total effect with the only aim to create the necessary atmosphere for the dance composition with his sets and to stimulate the spectator's fantasy with his costume designs. This circumscribes his task. His contribution is by no means an accessory, but it must never be dominant. The sets must be in harmony with the idea of the dance composition and they can undoubtedly lead to new choreographic ideas. The costumes must not only fit the dancer, but also—what seems even more important—the dance action, that is, the idea and the movements which express it.

Whether a ballet has a story or not, the controlling image for me comes from the music. Stravinsky's music had the most decisive effect on my work and has always made itself felt in the direction of control and amplification.

My first real collaboration with Stravinsky began in 1928 when I worked on *Apollon*. I consider this the turning point of my life. This score, with its discipline and restraint, with its sustained oneness of tone and feeling, was a great revelation to me. It was then that I began to realize that to create means, first of all, to eliminate. Not a single fragment of any choreographic score should ever be replaceable by any other fragment; each piece must be unique in itself, the "inevitable" movement. I began to see how I could clarify by limiting and by reducing what seemed previously to have multiple possibilities.

Although my work has been greatly linked to Stravinsky's music for a great many years, I do not feel that one specific style of music lends itself better to the projection of sound into visible movement than another. But it may be difficult to fulfill certain composers' personal inspirations.

What I mainly expect from the composer whose work I am to visualize is a steady and reassuring pulse which holds the work together and which one should feel even in the rests. A pause, an interruption, must never be an empty space between indicated sounds. It cannot be just nothing, since life goes on within each silence. It must, in fact, act as a carrying agent from the last sound to the next one. The secret for an adequate rendering of the musical score into visualization lies in the dynamic use of silence and in the utmost consciousness of time.

The composer is able to give more life to a bar, more vitality and rhythmical substance than a choreographer, or a dancer for that matter. The musician deals with time and sound in a highly scientific way, his medium of creation lends itself to a strictly definable method, to organization and translation of a formula into artistry.

It is far more complicated for the dancer to recite a formula. The choreographer will never be able to achieve such precision in the expression of movement as the composer through sound effect. Not that we do not know what we are doing. Our technique certainly has method, but it is far more interpretive than subject to mathematical rules. Whenever I feel I have found the "inevitable" movement, I can never be as sure as in music that it might not need some clarification after all.

In my choreographic creations I have always been dependent on music. I feel a choreographer can't invent rhythms, he only reflects them in movement. The body is his sole medium and, unaided, the body will improvise for a short breath. But the organizing of rhythm on a grand scale is a sustained process. It is a function of the musical mind. Planning rhythm is like planning a house, it needs a structural operation.

*Because people cannot see the color
of words, the tints of words, the secret ghostly motions of words:—
Because they cannot hear the whispering of words, the rustling of the
procession of letters, the dream-flutes and dream-drums which are
thinly and weirdly played by words:—
Because they cannot perceive the pouting of words, the frowning of
words and fuming of words, the weeping, the raging and racketing and
rioting of words:—
Because they are insensible to the phosphorescing of words, the fra-
grance of words, the noisomeness of words, the tenderness or hard-
ness, the dryness or juiciness of words,—the interchange of values in
the gold, the silver, the brass and the copper of words:—
Is that any reason why we should not try to make them hear, to make
them see, to make them feel? ...*   —LAFCADIO HEARN

———

CARMELITA MARACCI

The Symbolic and Psychological Aspects of the Dance

IN ANY appraisal of the dance today one should be aware of the
two elements which comprise this form of expression, the inward and the outward. The inward aspect of the dance, that
is the creativity of the artist, is at its strongest point of produc-
tivity; this in spite of the terrific outward pressure against keeping
alive an art form so specialized and so little understood, because
each dancer brings to it a very personal, and altogether subjective,
psychological approach. This is the American modern dance, not

in any wise to be confused with the more prevalent Freudian,
Daliesque ballet accomplishments. Symbolism in the former
reaches back to the Greeks; whereas in the latter, symbolic gesture
seems to spring in the main from efforts at browsing in the direction of Freud.

Though generalizations are dangerous, and I recognize exceptions, I believe that the over-all approach of the dance is derivative. Therefore, we cannot speak of the dance in America
without taking into consideration two distinct groups, the commercial ballet theater dance which, whether it feeds on private
capital or not, is a working organization that we, the audience,
can attend, or the non-commercial modern theater dance which
we can attend if we are privileged enough to be on the mailing list.

The psychological aspects of the American ballet are sometimes manifested in a decorative externalization, and it is much
more "fun" than the American modern dance which is dynamic
and troubled and not so much "fun."

The American modern theater dance suffers in greater proportion from the outward pressure than does the ballet theater
school. What is the outward aspect of the dance? It is the social-
economic circumstances in which each individual artist finds himself. The outward pressure limits, hinders, turns inward upon the
creative talent, and this in turn, like an ever-flowing flux, turns
outward to produce a strident trend of disturbance in expression.
The latter is conclusive proof of a kind of psychological frustration, and actually produces a dance which shocks present-day
audiences who do not recognize their own time, have no ceremonial attachment and have always felt the dance to be only a
diverting experience of no great importance.

This trend of disturbance is found in Mary Wigman as a
manifestation of the disillusionment of the post-World War
Germany of 1918 and later in America; it is the result of the age
in which we live, an age brought about by scientific discovery,
progress and social revolution. The American modern theater

dance is concerned, as much as is the scientist, with this changing world. The American ballet theater school is either stuck in the bend of the turn of the century's poetic niceties or concerns itself with grubby vulgarisms clothed in beach costume and phallic symbol décor. The wholesome American-scene dance is loved by both camps. The ballet treats it decoratively; the modern, with greater awareness as to the social and economic reasons as part of the pressing necessity of living. The latter school digs deeper and therefore is more dynamic than linear.

To make a general observation on the dance without mentioning names is, for me, impossible. The dance of Spain, for instance, we remember through performances of a few artists; and in the case of La Argentina, the greater the demand, the greater her outward success—and the less demand she felt to search for a true expression. Her glorious smile was the symbol to people of a sunny, carefree Spain. Commercialism in the dance is rarely a blood brother to creative awareness. In Argentina's case, people mistook her personality for representationalism. She was Spain. Because she danced few regional dances, her gesture had the grace of a diplomatic mission and she could be at ease in London, Paris or New York. Hers was the universal symbol; she was a lady, and a commercial triumph. Her wardrobe symbolized Paris; her dancing, the gardens of Spain; her bows, the envy of any Russian ballerina; and her gentility, that of an English lady. Argentina offended no one who could afford the price of a ticket. Argentina's dancing, therefore, was the genteel aristocratic symbol of a wilting social order. So individual and so subjective is dance expression that I have chosen, purposely, a Spanish dancer whose troubles were masked in an overwhelming smile. This was not a symbolic expression of Spain but rather a tasteful, acceptable expression of one woman's gentility. A dance so rooted in strict form was, strangely enough, an international diplomatic bow to our peace of mind. We still envy those who can afford champagne, orchids and all the other accoutrements of a special class. Argentina danced—what every woman wants—elegantly with the greatest degree of perfection. She was the essence of Spain if you could afford it.

The dance can only be a symbolic expression within the limitations of the individual's personal beliefs and his relation to society.

When we approach the symbolic aspects of the dance we must keep in mind the danger in connection with the use of symbol. For symbol in the dance is often misused to express something that is totally without coherence and arises out of a lack of information as to how to handle the symbols used. This misuse, in turn, brings forth confusion and a further reflection of "misrepresentationalism," as in the example of the Freudian ballets so prevalent today; in Argentina's case an unconscious use of superimposed meaning; the other—in the Freudian ballets—a conscious, half-baked use of symbol without adequate knowledge of the meaning.

The symbolic, contemporary American modern theater dance uses few symbols, relatively speaking, that can be understood nationally, even fewer universally. The import of such esoteric symbolism shrinks with the growth of a "one world" philosophy.

Symbols spring from antiquity, and the contemporary dance, unless it follows faithfully the direct purpose and fulfillment of ancient gesture, is weakened and loses its significance. Symbol is a telling shortcut to the written and spoken word. In antiquity, symbolic gesture was necessary for the understanding by large masses of their part in the spectacle and its relation to communal happiness. The barren expression of symbolism in our time was proven by the coincidental use or rather misuse of the first theme in Beethoven's *Fifth Symphony* as a symbol for victory. This is a dangerous clinging to antique methods of provoking mass excitement, in utter contrast to a genuine manifestation of symbolism.

Modern dance has concerned itself with primitivism much as the Left-Bank painters in Paris did with their jump back to African sculpture, and another jump to Japanese prints. Then it found itself confronted with the psychological genius of Freud. This is an unhealthy historical process. Natural historical progression was overlooked in ignorant sensationalism to provoke stylish response. The dance has not led. Its sycophancy feeds on literary, graphic and scientific trends. In the jump—a dynamic, frenetic, misdirected jump from antiquity to Freud—the American theater dance schools shockingly overlooked the evolutionary process. Nietzsche was fashionable. Isadora's bible, *The Birth of Tragedy*, was inherited by Martha Graham. Perhaps that is why Curt Sachs mentions only one dancer—Isadora Duncan—in his book on the history of the dance. In the past the dance was a leading art form, today it only follows other art forms. Isadora stripped away décor and elaborate costume, and gave to the dance the place it once held, that of an expression, in an art form, solely of the spirit. Her dance had a naturalistic simplicity closely akin to the great historical past.

The ballet brought people into a world of unreality or retreat, while the modern dance tried for a long time to bring people into the light of revealment. Prior to Freud, symbolic expression was subconscious, and with Freud, symbolic expression for the first time became conscious awareness as sexual expression of man's inner needs.

The dance remains more violently separated and more national than any other art form, mainly because it is not as highly developed as literature, music or painting. This lies in the fact that dancing has been—except in antiquity and where the dance is a necessary part of life in the community—a diversion to living, a theatrical tour de force. Work in progress for a dancer is polishing the bow without questioning the soul. We can go even further and say that the reason the dance is arrested is because it has forsaken its organic meaning, its joy in becoming. It is bogged down in meaningless symbols. The dance should not interpret words. It should discover and find, with humble questioning, and not feebly adhere with minimum effort to man's other mighty works. It isn't outside influence that warps the dance, it is the whole-hearted capitulation in blind, opportunist following of ignorance. If the dance is to assume any stature, it must spring forth from immediacy and embrace universal experience.

"Not the brow, but the experience; not the eyes, but the look; not the lips, but the sensuousness," said Spengler. The dance has been afraid of revealing the depth of human experience. The one art which could afford to be honest has preferred camouflage and confusion. I grant that the dancer reveals himself, and in many cases what he reveals he might well keep to himself. The problems that have beset more searching individuals are forgotten in the dancer's interest in his sex life. It is as if his coming of age was the most important and only event of his life. He can't get over it. This revealment concerns itself with murderous, incestuous, labyrinthine gloom, side by side with nasty, twitching, minute hands and feet studies. It is sodden, not soaring. It is knee-deep in the quicksands of gloom and fast sinking into total oblivion.

I am not in disagreement with this attitude except to find it a sorry situation if the artist feels at one with the spectator in projecting this despairing dance, and is shocked to find there isn't a large audience for it. Perhaps the audience's reaction, or lack of enthusiasm, for the psychological trend in the dance has provoked the dancer to turn more inward; this in turn has provoked, ironically enough, some enthusiastic response on its part, and the audience now considers sensationalism the important aspect of the dance and might regard more humanistic gentility with a scoff. Argentina would be old-fashioned. The danger in the dance field is its adherence to the prevalent mode. It is ashamed of heart and in the name of surgical dissection produces studies of personalized maladjustments. Granted this is the psychological age. Then why the renewed and ever-growing interest in chamber music, rooted as it is in romantic nineteenth-century thinking which embodies man's development up to Freud? Why, then, in this frayed-nerve period, the realization that we must do other than display our sickness without at least a working hope?

Albert Einstein and Thomas Mann, to name but two outstanding figures in the contemporary world, recognized the stringency of our times and the possible impending horror, and did seek through active participation to do what they could to pull us out of man's present dark dread of the future. We cannot think universally if our scrutiny is turned inward and we say: this is an interesting neurosis; all else is hopeless. It is hopeless if we are concerned with ourselves in one direction only, our sex life. Does the artist of today assume that Beethoven, Goethe, Goya hadn't any sex life? I think it is high time the dancers took it as part of living and realized that that is how we got past the nineteenth century, and let it go at that.

Even now it is old-fashioned to dance of possible better conditions. The New Dance Group's fist-shaking *Vanderloub's Head* is wearing a tutu these days. In the matter of muscular activity, they are neck and neck. Ballet dancers wear leotard, rubberized fishnet hose and ballet slippers; the modern dancer wears leotard and slippers. The ballet dancer is still more concerned with legs; the modern dancer with the torso. Both schools ignore the hands, but the face in the ballet department feigns sweet, sickly nausea, while the modern refuses to recognize the face as anything other than a nuisance with far too many unnecessary, busy interruptions of the fluid body-movement whole. But then you can't keep up with these things. What is fashionable at this very hour, I wouldn't know. I wouldn't be at all surprised if the ballet dancer had thrown away her toe-shoes and the modern dancer had caught them in mid-air and had found how delightful, if naive, it is to try to soar.

I don't wish to sound trite or malicious, but I have never felt that Martha Graham would have been greater in *Frontier* or *Primitive Mysteries* if she had been the product of the Cecchetti-Legat schooling. Nor do I feel that Escudero's *Farucca* would have benefited by the *entrechat ricaduta* or *ascendenza*. Not that the ballet dancer remembers that the pink slipper should only support the soaring, but unfortunately the toe-shoe is used as a crutch and a brace for almost anything but an ecstatic quality. In fact, there are many times when the modern dance could use to advantage (and has recently) a slipper, and many times when (*Saint Francis of Assisi, Facsimile*, etc.) the ballet could have—as in these instances—used the unshod foot to great advantage, or, in the second instance, at least recognized the implications of Freudian symbolism attached to the slipper. In the case of *Saint Francis of Assisi*, the incongruity of ballet slippers offended me as much as if one of the religious paintings of El Greco were to wink.

Specifically, the forms of the dance seem to restrict honest, good, straightforward approach in compositional method. Modern dance's approach to the *Sarabande*: long hemline, full bow to authenticity in the neckline and sleeves, to give you the feeling of the period, ruined by bare, calloused feet. To suggest country, if not always time, when the modern dance—in attempting Spanish themes as inspired by Lorca—presents a modern dance matador with knee-length tights (which he evidently finds comforting to his purse and his leotard technique), there is just a faint hint of costume so that we, the spectators, say, "Oh! Spain!" In the case of modern approach to female Spaniards, a piece of red cloth tied around an austere bun with perhaps a bit of rope rakishly placed to suggest a bolero is a sufficient bow in the direction of Spain. I have always been highly amused to find that four little pieces of wood and two pieces of string and shoes are never the accoutrements that modern dancers use in their comments or observations on Spanish themes. The American dancer dances everything and everybody.

The ballet dancer also loves Spanish themes on the more

sensational theatricalized level, because ballet dance stresses dexterity of feet. Ballet dancers can do rudimentary heel work rather rapidly; case in point is *Tricorne*. But again they use fancy hands instead of castanets. The ballet dancer's lack of dexterity of hands is equal to that of the modern's. The constant stress of *port de bras* and not *de mains* makes the ballet dancer forget that the hands are second only to the face as a means of fuller expression. Modern American Russian themes are done in the same manner, dispensing with extraneous detail. One likes to feel that this is a process of elimination rather than a lack on the part of the composer and executant. These works, when performed by the modern group, are done as a friendly expression of good will, but rarely are they as moving as when the modern dance adheres to its own American folklore or primitive dance movements. Such a highly integrated dance as the Spaniards possess will reach fruition, I hope, in a truly creative native Spanish dancer.

The ballet theater dance has not been concerned with Lorca, Goya, El Greco, friendly salutations to countries, but in a highly undisturbing way (unless you are as composed as I am) with a nod at past ballroom attitudes of these countries and their people. I mean, of course, the people in the ballrooms. The graduation balls; the lilac suffering of the privileged few; the flower-plucking pains of the maiden and a prince who suffers with her and after her; this never-ending theme and variation in a day when most of the world's royal courts have crumbled. Very seldom is this courtly obedience given a slap on the derrière. The one exception was Agnes de Mille's *Tally-Ho*. The latter may not have been a great work, but it had a point of view and was done by a person who didn't let slipper satin stand in the way of genuine comment and wit. Perhaps Miss de Mille understands her source material better than most dancers, and then invests her composition with a lively, provocative point of view. Perhaps it is best to say that Miss de Mille does not come from any single school of dance and never follows a cult-like formula which blinds most artists to the essential ingredient in any work of art: a wide comprehension of humanity, its frailties as well as its nobility.

On the one hand, the dance suffers from its derivative nature in its adherence to final formal pattern; on the other, from its separateness in that it does not join hands with the great developments of man. It is obedient to symbol insofar as its patience for research goes. It is hindered by fashion and its doubts are greater than its beliefs and it is afraid of its honesty. The modern dance is a truly successful form of movement-expression. It has lived inwardly so long because of the public's lack of interest that its contribution is of far greater importance than that of the ballet. Within the last few years it has admired the gloss of the ballet in a dangerous manner. So strong is the prejudice on the part of the public that managers call the works of the leading modern dancers "ballets." That the modern dance survives at all will be testimony to the genuine sincerity of the few who believe that the dance can do other than entertain.

It is a curious situation that in a country such as ours the dance has made such determined strides. It is a theatrical achievement in a country where folk dancing is kept alive by as small and determined a group as is the creative dance. This unhealthy situation is not the result of the dancer's ethics. The serious creative dancer survives despite public indifference towards an art expression it probably considers old-fashioned. The dancer, in many cases, has been forced to seek dance forms of other countries where such expression is a vital part of the people's lives. It is to be hoped that the rich vitality of the modern dance will not find its fate to be that of the folk expression of this country. Something so much a part of our times can live only if the participation of entire people is enriched by this earnest contribution.

Nothing so clearly and inevitably
reveals the inner man than movement and gesture. It is quite possible,
if one chooses, to conceal and dissimulate behind words or paintings
or statues or other forms of human expression, but the moment you
move you stand revealed, for good or ill, for what you are.

—DORIS HUMPHREY

RUDOLF LABAN

The Educational and Therapeutic Value of the Dance

LET ME say this at the very outset. The dance, as it is traditionally understood in our time, has no intrinsic educational or remedial purpose. The dance today is an art form which can be appreciated and enjoyed either as a spectacle, if performed by professional dancers, or as a recreational activity, if performed by laymen. Why its beauty and significance are appreciated and enjoyed is a question seldom, if ever, answered. Certainly, the answer will rarely include the mention of educational or remedial purposes.

The teaching of dancing or of the applied history of the dance in schools is desirable. As one of the subjects of education it can be compared with the teaching of other art subjects, such as music, painting, designing and modeling. Such teaching will enlarge the horizon of the pupil and will enable him to admire dances with more understanding. The adult having enjoyed art education and thus also dance education in his school days will be better prepared to use one or several of the arts for his recrea-

tional purposes with some taste and discrimination. The fact that
the dance is probably the primary art of man might give it a certain importance and preponderance over the other arts.

The oft proffered opinion that the dance is of educational
or therapeutic value, because it is the only art in which the human
being is involved as a whole, seems to me to be based on a mis-
comprehension. The fact that the dancer performs large and
clearly visible movements does not indicate at all that the whole
person is involved. I have seen many dancers who throw themselves into the air without any sign of inner participation. On the
contrary, such large movements are frequently very externalized,
comparable to hollow shells in which not the slightest indication
of an integration of body and mind can be discovered.

Yet there exists a part of the dance which, if purposefully
applied, can have an eminent educational and remedial value. It
will be expected that this part of the dance consists of nothing else
beyond the visible movement. The only trouble is that, although
highly valued and appreciated, it is rather difficult to catch its
real nature. What is the fascinating "something" which distinguishes the dances of a Pavlova from those of the members of her
company? Why are the star dancers and artists of the stage or the
screen so deliriously admired and able to earn fame and wealth?
Is it their outstanding technical perfection? No. Many acrobats
and acrobatic dancers can be found who have a far more highly
developed body technique than these idols of the public who, if
observed objectively, frequently do not show much more than an
average mastery of movement. Yet, they have this apparently indescribable "something."

We find this curious part or feature of movement in ordinary
life as frequently as we do in the art of dancing. Some people
move with a charm which is similar, if not identical, with that
of great artist dancers. Ordinary people do not associate their
charm of behavior with any acknowledged or unacknowledged
stage technique. They would never dream of dancing in a ballet

and yet, I am sure, they are quite conscious of and probably cherish and love the particular charm of their movement. They may even cultivate it. Now, if this is not the quintessence of dance I do not know what else it can be. Everybody who dances strives after this "something," even if sometimes unconsciously and perhaps clumsily. Dancers are often trapped by external skill which is indispensable for a theatrical career, but their guiding star is, without doubt, the charm of movement.

If one could call the humble striving after this radiant quality "dancing," I would have to refute my initial statement. I should have to affirm that the dance has the most eminent educational and remedial possibilities.

Because of its inexplicable influence on adolescents and its mysterious effects in healing certain illnesses, the dance was considered a magic art in remote epochs in the history of mankind. Present-day educationalists, addicted to fashionable intelligence tests, and doctors who believe passionately in drugs, might ridicule and despise the magic dances which to this very day permeate the education and medicine of the so-called primitive tribes.

The rediscovery of the dance as a means of education and therapeutic treatment in our time originated from the aesthetic pleasure which some teachers, doctors and industrial welfare workers took in watching modern stage dancing. They came to the dancers with the question: "Can you do this with our children, our patients, our workmen?" The dancers did it and with quite unexpected results. Not only did the children, patients and workmen enjoy themselves, but some of them seemed to be changed in an inexplicable manner by dancing. The headmistress of a school in which such dances had been arranged was surprised that a child, considered to be "dull and backward," suddenly became lively and interested even in intellectual studies. His sudden progress in such subjects as reading, writing and mathematics, where previously he had appeared hopeless, was astonishing.

Another remarkable fact was the improvement in the community spirit of whole classes. Cliques and solitary individuals, who had hitherto been competing and quarrelling tiresomely, became friendly and sociable.

A further surprising effect was that the health of some of the children improved. Weaklings who always had a horror of gymnastic exercises, and with whom drugs and other treatments had proved entirely ineffective, became stronger and more vital through dancing. Nervous children became less frightened, quieter and more open to advice and correction.

Now this might seem to be magic, since it cannot be explained. It took a considerable time to investigate the background of such effects. It has been observed that an old working woman, twisted by rheumatism, can have the essence of dance, this charm of movement, as well as a beautiful girl. A man can have it as well as a woman, no matter whether he is old or young. Moreover, this feature of movement can be acquired, developed, regulated and mastered. The only question is how, and this is a question deeply concerned with problems of education and recovery.

Education and remedial measures have a common factor; both have to deal with individuals who, through various causes, lack some inner or external qualities needed in the struggle of life. They must be helped to rediscover certain powers and functions. It is relatively irrelevant that education develops dormant qualities of a growing being, while remedial measures have to re-awaken qualities lost in the struggle of life. In providing powers and functions, both educational and remedial measures are greatly helped by the charm of movement.

Modern dancers, investigating this charm and seeking a new basis for their artistic expression and technique, took great trouble to study not only the external forms but also the deeper effort-content of working movements. Motion study in industry as first advocated by Taylor and his followers, protagonists of scientific management, awakened the keenest interest of modern dancers and found as much stimulation and help in them as they did in the exercises of traditional dancing.

The first occasion on which I could clearly see how dance and work were not only able but predestined to meet was a great pageant of crafts and industry, the organization of which was entrusted to me by the municipal authorities of Vienna. The idea was to call the attention, not only of the city and the country but of the whole world, to the great wealth of industrial tradition dying away in the aftermath of the First World War.

The task was a tremendous one, because all the working organizations, old and new, from the almost medieval guilds of handicrafts to the most complex groups of modern commerce and industry, felt it necessary to remind their contemporaries of their existence, their needs and their hopes. My idea of putting the rich traditions of industrial customs, and especially of the songs and dances of the crafts, in the center of the procession, soon caused it to be known as the dance procession of industries. It brought forth a wave of festive enthusiasm, the intensity of which surprised me.

Many thousands of different operations with all kinds of material and varying from the one-man shop to monster combines revealed to me their common denominator which was rhythmical effort in the flow of work, the charm of movement.

I learned to consider all the hammering, drilling, filing, assembling, transporting, as well as maintenance, repair, supply and distribution as one great unit, the overwhelming rhythm of which cannot be better described than as a symphonic ballet of human brain work and hand work.

The tragic background of this gay festival was the struggle— a life-and-death struggle—of people who were fully alive in their productive energy but had to face the rapid decline of all possibility of work. Craftsmanship was still cherished, and work, as far as it was available, was performed with real affection. On one

of the four hundred floats of the cortege a forge was installed and
the ancient methods of forging horseshoes in the Alsatian, Scottish
and Italian styles were demonstrated, each with its special rhythm
and accompanied by dances of apprentices and girls in similar
rhythms. Another float of gardeners and agriculturists showed the
origin of the well known Vienna Waltz, which is, as students of
the history of the dance surmise, the primeval threshing of corn
with the feet. Yet another float contrasted the bizarre old professional dances of medieval grocers with the gigantic rhythm of the
modern department stores. The factories—producing objects of
iron, glass, leather and all kinds of other materials—were represented by machine dances. The pride in work and the love of
perfect rhythmical performance was visible everywhere. The
whole festival revealed a gigantic poetry of movement and a traditional knowledge of the laws of motion ruling both dance and
work. Expressed, as it was, in living practice, it gave an excellent
example of how vocational education and recovery in festive recreation can be achieved through dancing.

We know today how primeval tribes accompany their work
with songs and dance-like body rhythms, and this old spirit is
by no means dead; movement training is at the root of almost
all industrial education, and, in a new form, it is the fundamental
idea of reformers like Taylor. In all the measures evolved to improve industrial efficiency, such reformers paid the greatest attention to human effort, without, alas, penetrating to the heart of
the problem of rhythm. For this reason they failed to introduce
its beneficial effect into contemporary work.

In earlier days when individual workers asked modern
dancers to help them improve their skill and relieve the strain of
their work it soon became obvious that the similarity between
popular dance forms and working procedures offered a valuable
basis for the study of the educational and therapeutic value of the
art of movement.

There are repetitive and free dance forms very like repetitive and free working movements. Although most repetitive work is done with arms and hands, and the dance with legs and feet, the movements require, as a rule, the same kind of inner efforts in both fields. In spite of the fact that the spirit of the dance is usually light and quick, while that of work is heavy and slow, and in spite of other similar differences in the use of the elements of effort, it soon became evident that exactly the same elements are used and combined in both work and dance.

The exercise of the complementary character of these two ways of moving is extremely salutary in its effects when working movements are taken as the basis of movement exercise, or artistic movements as a recreation and a stimulus for working people.

The workers seeking relief from the strain and pain of their work in the unique experience of the dance pageant, pointed unerringly to the unexpected but fundamental possibility of restoring lost energy and of improving working habits through the use of artistically harmonized movement.

Dancing, as a means of recovery from the strain caused by work, developed in much the same way as it did in schools. The only difference was that in the case of schools the teachers and heads of schools sought such advice and help, while managers and industrialists remained indifferent for a considerable time. It was actually the workmen themselves who, after seeing some performances by modern dancers, expressed the desire to do something similar. When they subsequently studied some dances selected for the purpose of recovery the result was the reduction of fatigue and pain in those parts of the body which were overstrained by repetitive activities. The workmen affirmed that they had become more interested in their work and especially in the rhythmical content of certain operational movements. Incidentally, a few charge hands, foremen and even managers joined in the dancing, but methodical application of rhythmic, dance-like exercises in the factory was a relatively later outcome. It was only

when workers' dance clubs and movement choirs had been established that this came about.

The study of the harmony of movement differs essentially
from the traditional technique applied to the performance of
some set steps. When man dances he may develop dormant as
well as lost qualities, just as occasion arises. He penetrates into a
realm of hidden treasures, some of which he may collect while
others he rejects or disregards. What are these treasures? Expressed briefly they are all experiences of the charm of movement.
Or shall I say they are valuable life experiences gained in movement? An example might make this clear.

Dance has often been used in olden times as a means of improving human relationships. Dance considered as a school of
behavior is expected to develop a deeper-rooted harmony of social
friendliness beyond external politeness. Our enquiring mind asks,
however, what is the mechanism of such achievement? This
mechanism might be revealed if we consider that people using
freely flowing movement become more open-minded than those
who are bodily cramped and wrapped up in themselves. This
opening is visible; when people gather together they can see and
discern more than the simple process of opening. They learn to
know one another through the reciprocal observation of their
movements. Traits of movements common to all human beings
are experienced and compared. Individual differences are noticed.
In everyday life certain peculiarities of movement may arouse
suspicion; aggressiveness, selfishness may be seen in them and provoke defense and aggression. Here, in communal dance, this fear
is abolished. There is no cause for immediate fight; fear is abolished, tolerance is awakened.

Such are the treasures discovered by the experiences made
in communal dance.

Individually, it is especially the control and mastery of one's
own movement which is felt to be beneficial, for fear and suspicion

are not restricted to the relationship with other people. One can be afraid or suspicious of oneself. Human behavior and its inner motives are surrounded by a great number of taboos and conventions which are apt to tint harmless inner stirrings with a shade of noxiousness or even danger. The self-conscious person is mostly not conscious at all of his self. Consciousness cannot be acquired by thinking alone. One must become familiar with one's own movements and the intentional stirrings mirrored by them. This familiarity is gained or, at least, promoted by dancing. To learn all these and many other similar things is without doubt an educational process. Dancing of the kind described has thus certainly an educational and perhaps even a therapeutic value.

The reluctance of some people to join in communal dances or to move freely for themselves cannot be exactly called an illness, but it is very near it. If the impregnation of suspicion with fear is too intense, so that a simple opening of the personality through free movement cannot take place easily, special forms of remedial dance exercises will be helpful. An adequate knowledge of human nature is an essential precondition for devising such exercises and dances. Here we come to the important question as to whether the dance teacher who wishes to apply his art to educational or remedial purposes can gain the necessary insight into human nature through his dance experience alone or whether he needs some additional studies.

The wealth of experience which dancing offers is illimitable. Yet, it is just this wide range which may be confounding. It is therefore a help to discern various types of dances. It is easily understood that dances of a more gymnastic or acrobatic kind might be of greater help in physical education and physical recovery than expressive dances which contribute to the education and the treatment of the emotional sides of man. It must, however, never be forgotten that dance in its deeper meaning involves both physical and psychic experience, though one of the two may prevail slightly in certain types of dancing. It is in any case not sufficient to subdivide dance steps into physical-acrobatic and psychic-expressive ones.

The methods to be developed for the application of the art of movement in education and therapy are closely linked with the recognition of the social aims of theatrical art. In recent years, institutions have been built up in which valuable research work dealing with contemporary movement habits is carried out. The training of artists, industrialists and teachers on parallel lines is undertaken in schools like the Art of Movement Studio of Lisa Ullmann in Manchester.

An important question is whether the theater of the future will be willing and able to follow the present trend of modern dancers and draw from the same sources of life which are becoming evident in our industrial civilization. In the first place, a greater consciousness of the importance of movement in the corporate effort in all works of stagecraft is needed. It should also be realized that the knowledge of the contemporary form of using movement differs greatly from the dance forms of ancient times.

The entertainment provided by the spectacular dance or the recreational pleasure of the dancing layman of our days is not sufficiently concentrated on the intrinsic features of the inner efforts and their conscious and purposeful application to human development and welfare. The educational or remedial effect of the dancing of today, if it ever arises, will be haphazard. In some individual cases the right effort might be awakened in the right person and at the right place. Yet how rarely this happens is shown by experience; otherwise all professional dancers would be perfect angels of an incredibly high level of inner balance and health. It cannot be too frequently repeated that it is nonsense to attribute to dancing itself any intrinsic educational or remedial value. It is the charm of movement for the sake of which dances are invented and selected which finally determines their effects.

Take, for instance, the motives behind traditional folk dances.

Every community that sets great store by pride of race and heroism will have dances which display proud and heroic gestures. These will be essentially different from the dances invented and cultivated by peoples of a languid or melancholic temperament. The ideal Spaniard, as figured in the dance imagination of his ancestors, will differ in many respects from the ideal Russian, as figured in Russian dance movements. So that dances show the difference in the racial idealization of personality.

The motives of which these dances consist are rhythmical sequences of efforts which can be considered as the phrases of the language of movement. The educational and remedial effect of dancing resides in whatever is expressed by such phrases of movement.

The educational and remedial value of the dance is often compared with that of sports and games. The movements in sports or games such as in the outstanding technique of tennis, football, hockey, etc., developed in England and the United States not so long ago; fencing in France and Italy. They show that a few typical efforts were cultivated and refined in these countries with no reference at all to those larger selections of rhythm contained in the national dances of, to name a few, Scotland, Russia, Hungary and Spain.

The rhythmical intelligence of the peoples who have a living tradition of communal dances is certainly of a higher order and their rhythmical repertory is far more comprehensive than that of peoples who have cultivated only sporting efforts. Dancing consists not only of more but of longer sequences of varying movements and efforts which distinguish it from games. The dancer must use his rhythmic ability during longer periods of time. He uses whole phrases of the language of movement, while the games player has in general only one cumulative action to perform—for instance, a hit—after which a pause occurs. The games player's effort-expression is not one of phrase or poetic sequence but of single exclamations.

Using the analogy of language, dancers are able to repeat certain poetic sequences and some of them are even able to use the entire vocabulary of rhythm in any desired combination. The dance is in this sense a rich and free poetry of movement, which can help to develop rhythmical intelligence and sensibility and thus bring man nearer to the physical and psychic balance of his capabilities. The disintegration of rhythmic sense frustrates all attempts to master life and the instinctive as well as intellectual desire to regain the lost rhythmicality is, partly at least, an appeal to the educative and therapeutic power of the dance.

Everybody has seen children jumping around happily. This might be considered as one of the natural forms of dancing. Children may even instinctively feel that their rhythmic jumping or dancing contributes to their bodily and mental well-being and to the development of some of their inner capacities and powers. This hidden self-education and self-remedy have both been studied and the knowledge acquired hereby forms an essential part of modern educational dance.

The performing dancer who exhibits an especially skillful variation of primitive jumping impulses is without doubt driven by the conviction of the deeper significance on the one hand in the recollection of his past experiences of exuberance from hilarity to sadness, and on the other hand in the anticipation of future excitements. A child can dance because of latent vitality, but can also dance in the expectation of food or of other pleasures in view. Sexual dances or war dances of olden times were anticipations of mating or killing. They produced without doubt an integration of bodily and mental functions which enabled the dancers to fulfill the expected activities with the whole power of their personality. It is, of course, a far cry from this primitive integration of function to the purposeful application of dancing in today's educational and remedial science. Yet, all we understand by the word "dance" today is, alas, mostly the rhythmic excitement of the child or of the man of primeval civilizations brought into skillful and aesthet-

ically interesting shapes which have no appreciable educational or
remedial influence in themselves.

The dance as a genuine means of education and recovery is
an entirely different proposition. The application of dance for
this purpose needs a special study of human nature and of the
inner efforts shown in movement behavior.

It seems as though racial memory preserves certain primeval
instincts such as were used and needed by man living in a virgin
forest. In our times such instincts are not really needed; industrial
man can survive without hiding himself behind symbolic behavior. And yet sometimes these old inherited instincts seem to
demand an outlet and appear then in the symbolic gesture of a
dance.

The wafting charm of Fokine's *Les Sylphides* may perhaps
be the expression of more domesticated instincts than those
shown in the demoniac impersonations of savage dances. Man
has many layers of inherited instincts in his body-mind and each
of these layers finds its expression in particular forms of movement. The most primitive layers might be mirrored in almost ani-
mal-like impulses, while the human and humane movements
surge from more recent deposits of racial memory. Older layers
are on the whole forgotten, even if they sometimes try to rise to
daylight.

The modern dancer tries to embrace the whole content of
all layers of the human psyche and this fact might explain the
liberating and therefore beneficial effect of this kind of dancing
on people in whom the various layers of the personality have become unbalanced.

It is the struggle of instinct-driven behavior, illustrating as
it does all the variations of human efforts, which forms the charm
and the real content of dances. This is also—so it seems—what
the modern psychiatrist might be able to use in curing certain
cases of neurosis. Some remote and primeval instincts dwelling

deeply hidden in man might give rise to movements which are an expression of the wild and almost indescribable frenzy typical of primitive races in their first savagery. Some movements might spring from the behavior inherited from a less remote and more domesticated ancestry. These ancestors might have cultivated certain social and individual virtues which could give rise to movements of a more gentle and less exaggerated type. We can learn much from the themes of the struggles and tales which we see on the ballet stage. Coming as they do from the depths of racial memory, they illustrate many of the finer shades of humorous and tragic moods in human behavior. In many ballets historical pictures are built up of periods of wild and reckless living in which the perversion of natural instincts is shown. In other ballets whole groups of dancers are transmuted into spirits. In *Les Sylphides* the wafting and floating of a whole company of ethereal dancers is brought into relief by one human who, himself, is lost in a dreamlike sea of emotional sentiment springing from the delicate instinct of tenderness.

It is not beyond the bounds of possibility that the line of development of the language of movement as well as of the ideas expressed in this language will lead to the scientific dance of a scientific epoch. The vision of the world as an arrangement of rhythmical vibrations on a vast scale of waves and dynamic streamings might prove a powerful incentive for future choreographers. Biophysical powers, effective in movement, will then be more consciously applicable to physical and mental recovery and regeneration through dancing.

Modern anthropology and psychology might provide as a background an amazing chemistry of the instincts underlying human behavior and of the transformation of their various manifestations throughout the ages. Today we know more about the human organism and its functions than in the days when the first dances were created.

But there is more to be considered than the present enlight-

ened view in regard to body and mind. For Art cannot be se
rated from Life, and the survival of the dance in everyday life is
one of the conditions for the survival of the dynamic arts as a
whole. It may be that well-meaning people who hate ballet might
be driven into this attitude because ballet, as they see it today,
appears to be separated from life. At least from life as they know
it, namely, the dreamless life of scientific man. One side of life—
the world of the dreamer—is so hidden from them that they can
no more see its meaning and beauty. But, if the question be asked
what happens to the minds of people who cherish the beauty of
the dream world, the reply will be that not only will such people
enjoy this beauty, but they themselves will contend that dream
life is the necessary compensation for the waking life. This opinion is, of course, one which is more commonly held in civilizations
other than ours. But amongst us can be found a few people who
see in the lack of coordination between the dream life and a waking life the cause of many of our individual difficulties and illnesses and cultural crises.

Love of the art of movement has a practical motive and it
is perhaps foolish of the artist to deny it and to hide the fact of
its usefulness behind the screen of pure aestheticism. There are
many comprehensible connections between dance and life and
one of these is the use of the art of movement as a means of education and therapeutics.

Keep in your souls some images of magnificence.

—ATTRIBUTED TO SEAN O'CASEY

———

PAULINE KONER

Pauline Koner Speaking*

TREND TO NOTHINGNESS

ARLY MODERN DANCE was an affirmation of life. Now it is a negation of life.

Early modern dance demanded the audience's emotional as well as intellectual participation. Now it is a visual experience which hypnotizes, and the audience responds with nothing—a blank acceptance.

Early modern dance was concerned with discovering human elements. Now it is discarding them.

The vitality of modern dance was its involvement in emotional, intellectual, and social problems. There was a sense of discovering and saying something of importance. What we had to say was vital to us; we argued about subject matter. Dance was a social manifestation. It was a seeking of life instead of an escaping from it.

Is life so difficult now that it is necessary to escape in order to survive? Escape is hardly a solution. Eventually whatever one is escaping from has to be faced. We must face life in all its emotions. The Roaring Twenties were a form of escape, but

---

* As told to Marcia B. Marks.

they were tame compared to now. Everything is intensified, more violent, ominous now—which is all the more reason to be involved with it. These are areas of investigation.

We must constantly re-evaluate. Values change, but the problems remain. The values of young people in the Thirties were different from those of today. They were living under the Depression and the threat of war. They could not face the future from an economic standpoint. Now the young people may have money but their psychological outlook is "Let's marry and have children fast because we don't know if we'll be here tomorrow."

West Side Story coped with present problems. It took a timeless theme and eternal antagonisms and conflicts and presented them from a different outlook.

Miss Koner questions the currently popular theory of "abstracting." What does this mean and why is it so important? Art must transcend the realistic, but transcending is not necessarily abstracting, and abstracting is not necessarily negating the human element. You can transcend without abstracting; you can abstract without transcending; and you can do both without negating the human element. We must transcend, yes —discard the extraneous—get down to the core, the seed. But to find the real core one does not abstract.

Doris Humphrey said to me, "Pauline, we must never forget what dance really means to us, what we are trying to say. We must never forget we are human beings—and what could be more important?" She feared this concept would not be fought for after she was gone, but anything great and important is timeless. What Isadora Duncan stood for and believed in remains—that the human form and human spirit are most beautiful and lasting. You cannot destroy the human spirit. Why deny it? Why throw it away?

Those who try to negate the human spirit—who will remember them? They are just a part of a passing trend. The only way one can know what is good or bad in art is what survives. During the past thirty years I have seen many things come and go, but I shall never forget Robbins' *The Cage* and Tudor's *Pillar of Fire* and *Lilac Garden*, because they moved me. So many dances leave one untouched, unmoved. A dancer should be able to raise an arm and make someone cry—in the way Isadora Duncan did. It is a necessity for any art to move you. You should take away from a performance something that lives with you. Now you see things that are fascinating, that make you vibrate, but when you leave the theater, you leave them behind. They do not make you different. Modern dance used to do this. It is important to be illuminated, transported. The technique may be brilliant—but so what?

THE DANCER'S TRAINING

The perfect attitude toward teaching dance is to train the body to move in every possible way. If each limb is trained to its maximum potential, the body can lend itself to any style.

For a basic technique, however, hunks of ballet, modern, Oriental, or other dance forms should not be lumped together in a hodgepodge. Instead the special characteristics or qualities of each form of dance should be incorporated in a basic technique without resorting to the actual exercises of any particular discipline. The dancer should be capable of the precision, speed, and turnout of ballet, the eloquent gestures and effortless movement of Oriental dance, the elegant carriage, emotional intensity, dynamic contrasts, and rhythmic patterns of Spanish dance, the complex rhythms of jazz dance, the isolations of African body movements, the undulations of the Hawaiian hula. The possibilities are infinite; the need is to break away from the restrictions of specific techniques to concentrate on the instrument itself.

With a perfectly trained body, the dancer's unlimited range

will make it possible for him to adapt to any style at all in a very short time. He will not be like the ballet dancer, completely turned out, nor like the modern dancer, now partly turned out and partly turned in, but will be a dancer who can completely turn out and completely turn in. (The Javanese dancer, whose walk is a deep in-out movement of the foot and leg, has had this facility for centuries.)

Much of what Miss Koner emphasizes in her own classes can be traced back to her early studies. Remarking that "few teachers today teach 'dance,'" she speaks of Fokine as one whose teaching went beyond technique. I learned the poetry of dancing with Fokine—a poetic line of movement, a poetic line of thinking, drama, the harmony of the whole, phrasing. She believes a teacher should train her students to think in terms of a phrase even when performing an exercise. Sometimes simply an extra breath finishes off a phrase. She finds that many of today's dancers have either forgotten or never been exposed to the breath phrase, or suspension, and rebound, the particular elements from which Doris Humphrey evolved so much of her movement.

To make students see that the quality of dance must never be lost, even in the mechanics of studying technique (otherwise dance becomes mere acrobatics), she suggests giving short studies on particular exercises. Suppose the subject is speed or fluidity. She develops the theme by varying the movement, the rhythm, and the emotional color. At the same time the students become aware of floor patterns and space relationships. She has found that studies like these are not only provocative in loosening the dancers' imaginations and limbs but excellent in preparing them for the time when they will need to learn a dance quickly on the job.

At some point within a movement—at the beginning, toward the middle, near the end, depending on the movement's emotional and artistic motivations—she changes the impact and increases the vitality by means of a pulse. The term pulse, or point of pulse, is used in preference to accent, emphasis, or stress, because it best conveys the idea of a development from within the movement itself without loss of continuity.

THE ELEMENTS OF PERFORMING

In teaching, Miss Koner isolates the elements, discusses their ingredients, and then combines them. In this way she tries to stimulate the students to a greater awareness of the art of performing and encourages them to search and experiment on their own.

According to Miss Koner, emotion and motivation should exist in all dance, no matter how "abstract." The first often becomes the second—that is, emotion or mood being the motivation of movement. These subjects can be explored in themselves, or they can also be introduced simultaneously with the study of focus and dynamics.

Emotion and motivation need not, of course, be related to characterization, since they appear in pure dance, too. But the creation of a three-dimensional characterization requires understanding of not only the primary but also the secondary elements.

Focus is the first essential among the primary elements. Its basic definition as "a center of awareness; a central point; a center of activity, attraction, or attention; a point of concentration" encompasses its many specific facets.

Focus exists simultaneously on several levels. Most important is Inner Focus, which must at all times coordinate with any of the other forms of focus. It is expressed in an awareness of the specific intensity of an emotional quality and in concentration to such a degree that one is not aware of the audience as individuals but only as a collective presence. It is this concentration and not the much-touted "projection" which a dancer must learn in order to reach an audience. "It is not the artist who goes out to the audience; it is the audience which is invited to share the experience on stage."

Performers trying to sell their own personalities to the audience project, but the artist is so involved with the substance of his performance that he is able to illumine. Sometimes the substance, such as comedy, demands direct audience contact, but this is motivated by the material, not the performer.

Rather than "projection" the word should be *magnetism*, and this is achieved by the power of concentration.

> You feel a vibration, a blue flame, an electric current between you and the audience which must be kept in constant play. You must have the capacity to receive and absorb as well as give. It is your concentration, awareness, and sincerity that spark the current.

> Before you make your entrance you are like a racehorse, poised, tuning your vibrations to a higher, finer pitch. It takes infinite discipline to achieve this concentration, but it is the very essence of performing. Before the curtain goes up, you must be completely involved.

Another form—Space Focus—splits into *directional*, *area*, and *magnetic* focus.

Directional focus is concerned with the "points of attention"—the concentration of the eyes and mind on a specific point in a specific direction (forward, back, up, down, and variations and combinations of these) or on a continuously moving point (following a bird in flight). Miss Koner bids, "Do not stare, but look; do not only look, but see." A simple example of directional focus is the man standing in the street looking up who draws a crowd around him. It is the same with an audience; they follow where you look.

Area focus involves "areas of awareness"—the concentration of the eyes and mind to encompass a specific area. The "area of solitude" gives a sense of complete isolation on stage, and though one may move anywhere on the stage, the sense of complete aloneness remains. It is an inner, emotional focus. The "area of the stage" gives a sense of space which isolates the stage from the auditorium. Your world remains within the edges of the stage. The "area of the auditorium" gives a sense of space which steps beyond the stage and includes the theater. Your world is now larger than just the stage area. The "area of horizon" gives a sense of space which reaches beyond the walls of the theater as far as the horizon. The "area of the sky" gives a sense of completely open space.

Magnetic focus establishes a focal point through use of the body instead of the eyes, creating a sense of being impelled toward a certain point or area. For example, reaching toward one point while facing another.

A third focus, Dramatic Focus, can be realized in many ways. One essential is to be aware of other people as people and not as things. Another is to relate oneself both physically and emotionally to the other dancers through the characterization and situation. It is also possible for a solo dancer to people the stage by use of strong points of attention.

The final focus is Body Focus, which creates a heightened awareness of a particular part of the body, forcing the attention of the viewer to some specific point on the body. For example, the violent head rolling in African dance or the continuous use of the elbow to lead an arm movement.

Focus soon becomes a reflex action for students, and they find themselves making use of it even in technique class.

Dynamics is an element of performing that is not always easily understood. It is the use of varying gradations and relationships of time, intensity (emotional and muscular), and space range. The gradations extend from the smallest to the greatest. Time varies from slow to fast; emotional intensity, from gentle to powerful; muscular intensity, from weak to strong. Space range, which applies not only to the whole body within its spatial area but to each part of the body, varies from small to large. (For instance, the complete area that an arm covers in circular movement has a much greater space range than the area covered by a circular movement of the head, so that a *small* circle of the arm might equal in space range the *largest* circle of the head.)

Dynamics may involve any one element or a combination of elements. The use of one may automatically introduce the use of another, but the gradations will not necessarily parallel each other. For instance, the tempo could be very fast—at its maximum in the dynamic range—yet the emotional intensity gentle —at its minimum—as in a very lyric run. Transitions are achieved by crescendo (a gradual increase of any or all of the dynamics), diminuendo (a gradual decrease), or sudden change (an unexpected shift from one gradation to another).

After exploring the primary elements of performing, Miss Koner introduces the secondary elements.

Props are considered in terms of their technical handling, function, associations, and symbolical possibilities. There are stage props (levels, steps, ramps, drapes), large mobile props (chairs, ladders, screens), hand props (fans, ropes, sticks, swords), and cloth in varying sizes and textures. By investigating the potentials, very often the student can discover a new area of movement. One student in a study on Mary, Queen of Scots, made symbolic use of a fan to represent first the queen's collar and then the axe.

The study of costume, both ethnic and period, can give a consciousness of style. Thorough analysis of the design and construction of a costume creates an understanding of the movement possible within it. This knowledge, used properly, helps retain the flavor of a style no matter how contemporary the movement may be. The dancer can learn how to move well in a skirt, and how a skirt can be handled to represent a child in her arms or a shawl over her head. In working with cloth, the dancer should know about the mechanical handling—its tension, weight, sound—as well as its symbolical possibilities.

Stage mechanics includes a variety of detail: bows, entrances and exits, space awareness (one's relationship to other people on stage and to the stage itself), awareness and knowledge of light (how to know the "hot spot" of the light), rehearsal problems, emergency situations.

All of these elements combine in a great performance. The infinite detail that makes of performing an art, and makes of the performer an artist, is both the obsession and the magic of the theater. The resources outlined in this article are keystones. They have been proved—they need only to be used.

Music written for theater, that is, to accompany danced or sung action, has certain limitations not shared by other music. While in one sense music is the most important initial feature of dance, inasmuch as it serves as root-rhythmic base, it cannot exceed a certain point of importance without competing with the action for which it is composed. Theater-music is intended to order and emphasize the activity in spectacle. It is music with a "program"; it indicates and describes for the ear what the eye sees. Its description is frequently far from literal. There is visual as well as aural counterpoint. —LINCOLN KIRSTEIN

———

NORMAN LLOYD

Composing for the Dance

THE FORMS OF THE DANCE

DANCE, like music, takes many forms. Some of these forms are in the realm of social dance: folk dance, jazz couple-dances, waltzes, Latin American tribal dances. The impact of social dance music—medieval estampies, Renaissance and Baroque court dances, nineteenth-century national dances, jazz—on so-called "serious" music is a field of study that could serve as the basis for any number of Ph.D. theses.

In the realm of theatrical dance there are the dances that entertain the tired businessman in a night club; the spectacle dances in opera and musical shows; the pleasant, the lyrical, the ecstatic, the storytelling, the abstract, the message-bearing dances of contemporary ballet and modern dance companies.

Dance is, above all, a form of theater. And like theater it is unpredictable. Each new dramatic situation demands a new solution. The composer who writes for dance views each dance as a set of new problems presenting several possible solutions. His skill as a composer for dance lies in his ability to choose one of the correct solutions.

THE COMPOSER AND THE CHOREOGRAPHER
OR, HOW DANCES ARE MADE

The story of the collaboration between composer and choreographer is seldom told. In musical autobiographies it usually takes the form of: "And then I wrote. . . ." In dance there has been no way of transmitting choreography except by means of person-to-person teaching. Dance has not had a written language until quite recently. As a result, we have the musical score for the first ballet—but no idea of what happened in movement. We read about the marvelous dance patterns created by Beauchamps (after watching a flock of pigeons) for the ballets of Molière and Lully—but we do not know how the dancers moved. We wonder in vain about the shocking dancing of Marie Sallé and Fanny Elssler. We shall never know what it was like. It is tantalizing to study Beethoven's one ballet, *The Creatures of Prometheus*, and speculate about the movements designed by the great genius Viganó. Even the recent trilogy of dances by Doris Humphrey—*New Dance*, *Theatre Piece*, and *With My Red Fires*—with marvelous music by Wallingford Riegger, have not been notated. Yet these dances came closer to truly "symphonic" proportions than any dance in the past twenty-five years.

But even without knowing too much about the dances of the past, it is possible to categorize the ways in which dance and music come together.

Jean Erdman has contributed to the modern dance with an equal measure of emotional fervor and intellectual probing. Seen here in *Duet for Flute and Dancer* and in her successful stage version of *Finnegans Wake* entitled *The Coach With the Six Insides*

Photos by Walter Daran (Duet) and Bernard Simon (Coach); courtesy of Jean Erdman

In most cases the dancer has been thinking about his project for a long time. When he finally has arrived at what he believes is the final version of his dance idea, he presents the composer with a scenario. Sometimes the scenario is just a bare statement of a story or mood line. The dancer might have thought of how many minutes he wants in each section. But there is elasticity to his plan. The composer can write a bit more or a bit less than the time allotted to him. The dancer might have specific types of movement in mind for the various sections of the work. These movements often give the composer indications for tempo, dynamics, or even melodic form.

On the other hand, the choreographer often goes to great length to describe what he wants the composer to do. A composer working on a long ballet received a letter from the choreographer, who was on tour (many dances have been composed by correspondence). The letter, four tightly packed pages of handwriting, told the composer all the thoughts that were to be suggested by the music as a character in the ballet walked slowly across the stage. It told all the inner thoughts of the character, pointed out his psychological problems, flashed back over his past life, and brought him up to the present. And all of this had to happen in a comparatively short musical time.

Choreographers are not always so explicit about the motivation of their characters. But they are often most precise in other ways. Petipa, great choreographer at the Maryinsky Theater in St. Petersburg (Leningrad), gave these detailed instructions to his composer, Tchaikovsky:

> Soft music . . . 64 bars. The tree is lit up . . . 8 bars of sparkling music. The children enter . . . 24 bars of joyful animated music. A few bars of tremolo depicting surprise and admiration. A march . . . 64 bars. A short rococo minuet . . . 16 bars. A galop. Drosselmayer, the magician, enters . . . awe-inspiring but comic music . . . 16 to 24 bars. The music changes char-

acter during 24 bars, becoming lighter and gayer. Grave music for 8 bars. A pause. Repeat the 8 bars. Another pause. Four bars expressing astonishment. A mazurka . . . 32 bars. A strong rhythmic valse . . . 32 bars.

That out of these instructions came the music for the *Nutcracker Ballet* is a tribute to Tchaikovsky's genius—a genius which enabled him to write three of the greatest scores for dance.

Jean Georges Noverre, whose *Letters on Dancing* (1760) served as the basis for most later developments in dance, collaborated with Gluck on the ballet for *Iphigenie en Tauride*. He explained to Gluck how he wanted each phrase of music to be written so as to fit each step, gesture, and attitude.

This approach is similar to that of many of the modern dancers who were working from 1930 to 1950. The dancer created the entire dance first. Then the composer was called in. He looked at the dance, notated its general form, its phrase structure, its metric pattern, and often the note patterns used by the dancers.

The composer's problem was to write a piece of music that would fit the dance like a tailor-made suit. The dancers and the composer had frequent meetings to "try on" the music. Changes were often made and even whole sections of the music were discarded and the composer told to try again. At times the job of the composer was more like that of a sausage-stuffer. An exact amount of music must be stuffed into an exact amount of time. As dancers discovered that their musical scores suffered by such a procedure, they gradually returned to the traditional scenario, allowing a certain amount of freedom for the composer.

With very few exceptions—mostly Stravinsky—no composer has instigated a successful ballet. The moral of this random thought is that a composer should find a dancer who has an idea for a dance—unless one is Stravinsky.

A FEW PERSONAL NOTES

There are times when composer and choreographer collaborate. Doris Humphrey had the notion of making a dance to Garcia Lorca's poem "Lament for the Death of Ignacio Sanchez Mejias" for José Limón. She asked me to write the music. We began by discussing the idea for at least half a year until we began to have a sense of the form and style that the work would take. We decided that I should write the music for the opening and closing sections of the poem while Miss Humphrey would work out the big dance section in the middle of the piece.

After several weeks we came together, I to play the music, she to show me her dance. We changed creative places, and I went to work on the middle section while she began to choreograph the beginning and ending.

We met constantly. As we put the work together we (more correctly, "she") saw that the beginning was too slow in getting started. Miss Humphrey correctly surmised that after the curtain went up, the music had to have the same impact as the opening tableau. We tore the music apart, rearranged its sections, and ran the piece through again. Much as I hated to have my music lose its leisurely build-up, I had to admit that her theatrical sense was right.

The total length of time spent in planning and composing the work—about one year.

José Limón's La Malinche was written in thirty-six hours.

La Malinche was scheduled to have its premier in Boston on a Wednesday. Exactly a week before, the composer who was supposed to be writing the score confessed that the job was too much for him. After all, twenty-five minutes of music is a lot of music to write.

José called me on the phone. The situation was desperate. The dance was completely finished and was needed for the program. Would I try to knock out something? For an old friend I would.

After finishing my teaching on Thursday afternoon, I went downtown to the dance studio where José was rehearsing. I took with me a big batch of manuscript papers. The dancers—José, Pauline Koner, and Lucas Hoving—performed the work for me. I took in the general quality of the piece. Next we worked phrase by phrase. I drew bar lines on manuscript paper, notated accent, cadences, and any important dance rhythms. José sang for me the trumpet calls used by the Mexicans in their revolt against the Spaniards. I went home, wondering how to approach the problem. The story was that of the betrayal of the Mexicans by La Malinche, an Indian girl, who helped Cortez. La Malinche, an eternal symbol of the traitoress, eventually rouses a dormant Mexican (Limón) to overthrow the arrogant Spaniard (Hoving). The whole dance had a folk-play quality.

I started writing Thursday night. To simplify matters I decided to use a "village band" sound of trumpet, drums, and piano. From there it was easy to identify the trumpet with the Spaniard, the drums with the Mexican, and a soprano voice with La Malinche. Contrapuntal or harmonic subtleties were out. There was no time to write much music.

A gay little Mexican folk tune served as the basis of the beginning and ending to the work, as the strolling players paraded on stage and, at the end, took their bows. I sat down and wrote for thirty-six hours, filling up the paper with the stipulated amount of music. After a short nap I took the sketches in to the rehearsal studio. We "tried on" the music. With a few minor adjustments it fit, thanks to the great musical understanding and absolute rhythmic precision of the three dancers. I went home, had another nap. Then the music was written in score. Saturday afternoon it was in the hands of the copyist. And on Wednesday night, on schedule, it had its first performance.

HINTS AND RANDOM SUGGESTIONS

The most basic rule for dance music is: if it works, it's good. This has little or nothing to do with the quality of the music as music. A dance score cannot be judged on purely musical terms. It is necessary to know what is happening on the stage in order to judge the true effectiveness of the music. Dance music is not just an accompaniment—but neither is it the whole show. Dance, like all theatrical art forms, calls for a blending of movement, sound, lights, costumes, and stage sets. The value of a dance score lies in its contribution to the total theater form.

This is not to say that dance music cannot be good enough to be listened to as music. Much of it is. But some dance music completely right for the dance, does not lend itself to an independent existence, any more than does the piano part of a Schumann song.

The most effective theatrical sound is a snare drum roll. It creates suspense, heightens the excitement of the moment, and has little or no musical value. The same is true of much dramatic music, such as the frightening sounds created by Carl Maria von Weber in the "Wolf's Glen" scene of *Der Freischütz*. The score for most Hollywood cartoons is absolutely right when heard with the picture. Away from the picture, the score is likely to be a series of disconnected short phrases interspersed with musical "Pow," "Crash," and "Yeek."

Most satisfactory dance music seems to be built sectionally. Dance seems to call for musical phrase placed in correct juxtaposition, rather than for symphonic emotional sequences. The master of such sectional writing is, of course, Stravinsky. The score of *Le Sacre* is full of contrasts of tonality, dynamics, orchestration, and rhythm. But there is no attempt to modulate, with the feeling of going somewhere that modulation implies.

Good dance music does. Much good symphonic music is involved with becoming.

A dance seen recently was defeated by its accompanying score. The music rose to climaxes, surged passionately, and developed its material skillfully. But one looked in vain for anything in the dance that called for such an array of musical forces. As a result, the dance was made to look more pretentious than it really was. The moral here is that too little is better than too much. After all, dances have been performed effectively without any musical accompaniment. (A good example is Doris Humphrey's *Water Study*.)

In line with the above, dance music does not have to move a great deal to be effective. The brooding opening of William Schuman's *Night Journey* and the bland but warm beginning of Aaron Copland's *Appalachian Spring* give the audience a foretaste of the mood of the dance that is to follow. Such fairly static sounds also allow the watcher to take in the stage set, the lights, and the costumes of the dancers. There is a kind of metaphysical "space" that cannot be filled too completely. Music that is too active crowds out the other sensations. There must be "space" for the dance. A beautiful example of such "space" is that left by John Cage's few assorted noises that are coincident with Merce Cunningham's *Antic Meet*. The hilariously funny dance makes its points in purely dance terms. The "music" does not get in its way. It is possible that music that tried to be as funny as the dance would call too much attention to itself. And nothing is less funny than a performer saying to the audience: "Look, folks! I'm being funny!"

FIVE DANCERS—FIVE INSTRUMENTS?

Every now and then there is a discussion about the relative number of dancers and musicians. "Does it seem right for a whole symphony orchestra to play for one dancer?" "Can a large dance company be moved by the sounds of two instruments?" These questions reflect a complete lack of awareness of the problem of combining sound and movement. One of Martha Graham's most contrapuntal group dances was *Celebration*. The stage was active with dancers jumping, falling, and weaving intricate patterns. A score which mirrored the complexity of their movement would have reduced the total effect to pure chaos. Instead, Louis Horst wrote a score for trumpet, clarinet, and drum. The music for much of the time was a single melodic line with a drumbeat to hold the dancers together. There was enough music to provide a mood background of celebration— but not so much music that there would be interference.

The opposite approach was used by William Schuman for Martha Graham's solo *Judith*. In this work Schuman utilized all the resources of the symphony orchestra to provide the stormy, terrifying atmosphere for the dance. Many purists—of music or the dance—criticized the work on the dogmatic ground that one dancer does not need sixty to ninety musicians. Most of these people would not be critical of Mozart because he used but one soloist in his piano concertos.

The truth is that the composer must use the number and type of instruments that he thinks will be most effective for the work at hand.

THEATER, INCLUDING DANCE, IS THE PLACE TO EXPERIMENT

The history of musical theater and ballet has shown us that many new sounds have come into general usage via the orchestra pit: the oboes in Lully's operas; the clarinet, trombones, and "Turkish" percussion instruments in eighteenth-century operas; the tubas in Wagner's operas. The experiments in music today are those involving nonmusical resources: the tape recorder and the electronic gadgets. Dancers have been most receptive to the new ideas for sounds. The orchestra of Haydn–Berlioz–Strauss is usable for many musical ideas. It does not necessarily provide the instrumentation needed for dramatic situations of today. The dancer or playwright who is concerned with the problems of living in a world of outer space, automation, crowded living conditions, canned foods and canned news, eruptive political events, Existentialist thinking—the list could go on—his musical needs will not be taken care of only by the sweet sound of violins.

The music of Varèse was used by Martha Graham and Hanya Holm long before it became popular in the concert hall. Doris Humphrey's *Theatre Piece No. 2* showed the dramatic possibilities of the electronic music by Otto Luening and Vladimir Ussachevsky. George Balanchine and Alwin Nikolais have made electronic music the basis of several exciting dance compositions. Merce Cunningham has used John Cage's "prepared" piano as well as the sounds of what might be called his "unprepared" orchestra. There is no sound that cannot properly be used in the theater.

TO BE "ETHNIC" OR NOT

A critic once said to me: "Why did you write dissonant, contemporary-sounding music for a dance about something that took place in Mexico in the 1800s?" My answer was that the work was not a costume drama but a conflict between two men and two antagonistic ways of thinking.

In handling historical material in dance, the question always is: How important are the locale and the time? If they color the dance they probably must color the music, at least to some extent. But it is possible to suggest primitivism without writing authentically primitive music (*Le Sacre*) or America of the pioneer days without quoting liberally from *The Bay Psalm Book*. Strangely enough, the purist-critic never asks if *Tristan and Isolde* is based on Irish folk melodies, or Gluck's *Orfeo* on authentic Greek tunes.

Pearl Lang, a former member of the Martha Graham Company, is a lyric and dramatic dancer whose poetic images are precise and meaningful. Her works are organically conceived and apply intellect and emotion with equal intensity. Shown here in *Song of Deborah*

Photo by Walter Strate; courtesy of Pearl Lang

IS THERE A LIMIT OF COMPLEXITY
FOR DANCE MUSIC?

Dancers have made successful dances to every kind of accompaniment. But there is one general rule about complexity that seems to hold true: The more dancers there are on stage, the more apparent must be the pulse of the music. This does not mean that dancers cannot dance to music where the pulse is subdivided fourteen different ways nor that they cannot cope with constantly changing meters. But there must be a definite pulsation if a large group is moving.

One of the primary functions of dance music is that it is needed to hold a group of dancers together, just as any marching group needs a drumbeat or a spoken cadence. A solo dancer can be out of step with the music of a complex score and no one (including possibly the dancer) would be the wiser. But with almost forty dancers on stage, it does matter if the dancers are out of step with each other. There is a point of rhythmic subtlety beyond which the composer cannot go. He must constantly have in mind the fact that his music has a kinetic function as well as an emotional or mood-making function. Successful dance scores do have a clearly perceptible beat, despite the seeming complexities of the music. One has only to listen to *Le Sacre du Printemps*, *Swan Lake*, *Appalachian Spring*, or Schuller's *Symphony for Brass* as used by Limón in *The Traitor*. Labyrinthian or not, there is always a feeling of pulsation.

For more than twenty-five years, Louis Horst and I have taught music composition for dance at Bennington College and the Connecticut College School of Dance. Our first advice to young composers is always: "Show the dancer how much time elapses from count one to count two." Once the pulse is established, the composer can indulge in all kinds of syncopations and other rhythmic tricks.

SHOULD MUSIC IMITATE GESTURE?

Since Rameau first wrote sweeping passages during which nymphs ran across the stage or descending scale patterns while the gods descended from on high, composers have attempted to introduce gesture into music. The effect is sometimes dramatic —and oftentimes ludicrous. In opera such musical pantomime defeats the very purpose for which it was planned. When Wagner writes spear-flourishing music for Wotan or draught-downing music for Siegmund, the double statement is almost too much. And when the music says to the audience: "Listen to me bow my head while the soprano does the same," the magic of theater is lost and embarrassment sets in.

Even a dance which uses dramatic incidents throughout does not have to be handled like a Walt Disney cartoon. (The process of musical imitation of something visual is known in the trade as "Mickey-Mousing.") José Limón's *Moor's Pavane* tells all the important actions in the story of Othello. But it is set against the highly formal music of Purcell. Dance music and dance movement coexist, but they do not have identical functions. If the dance is going to tell the audience exactly what the music is saying, then there is no need for the dance. The same is true of music; sound must add something to the visual event. At the beginning of Martha Graham's solo *Frontier*, she slowly raised her arm to a position above her head. The obvious musical solution was to write music that also rose slowly. But Louis Horst caught the emotion behind the movement and wrote music which opened a vista of the American plains that the dancer was viewing. The dancer's arm moved slowly; the music was active, quivering with excitement. Such is the ideal counterpoint of music and motion.

A genuine dance notation is the representation through the use of symbols, of ideas which are expressed by movement. The fact that the content of movement becomes understandable through its shape and rhythm is not surprising, since all that we can really see . . . in movement is its shape and the relationship between shapes as they follow one another. —RUDOLF LABAN

ANN HUTCHINSON

The Preservation of the Dance Score through Notation

HISTORICAL BACKGROUND

MUCH HAS been written on the development of dance notation through the ages, and the merits of one system versus another, but little has been said about the dance score as such. This is largely due to the fact that, with few exceptions, no system has been in use for a sufficiently long time or by a sufficient number of people to leave proof of its value in the form of completed dance scores.

The manuscripts and books which have been handed down through the centuries are the source of our knowledge of the dances of former times. Though much can be done through words and pictures, the contributions in the form of different notations, those of Feuillet, Zorn and Stepanov to mention a few, are invaluable. As Gaspare Angiolini, a contemporary of Noverre, said:

"Feuillet did more for the future by recording some of the dances in notation than Noverre, who failed to do so."

There is truth in this, but we are nevertheless indebted to writers like Arbeau, Noverre, Rameau and Blasis, who gave us such a clear insight into the thought and feeling of the day concerning the dance. Thanks to Arbeau, we know about the Basse dances of the sixteenth century. We also have many examples of the court dances of the time of Louis XIV due to the widespread use of Feuillet's system of notation, in which many suites of dances were published in different countries. During the nineteenth century Zorn perfected the notation system started by St. Leon, and published many examples of folk dances and ballroom dances of the time, the best known being the minuet. While these notations are sketchy—Zorn, for example, often took it for granted that the reader was familiar with the steps and so would omit a turn or other necessary detail—researchers have been able to reconstruct them. With a knowledge of the music and costume of the period and an understanding of the behavior of the people through study of the contemporary literature and painting, we can reconstruct the dances with a degree of authenticity.

Among the people well known for having so reconstructed the old court dances are Melusine Wood and Arthur Mahoney. Miss Wood has devoted years to research into the costume, music, ideas and behavior patterns of the day in order faithfully to reconstruct the movements. Mr. Mahoney studied the Feuillet manuscripts in Paris, and has since given many performances of the court dances of the seventeenth and eighteenth centuries. A recent example was the complete ballet he choreographed to Handel's score, entitled *Parnassus*.

The first complete ballets on record to be written in a dance notation were those in the Russian repertoire written in St. Petersburg by Stepanov. The notation of *The Sleeping Beauty* was used when it was later revived, the most recent instance being the revival for the Sadler's Wells company.

CONTEMPORARY SYSTEMS OF NOTATION

Of the more recent attempts to devise a workable notation, few are still in existence and even fewer have left any dance records of value. Little if anything is being done in the Margaret Morris movement notation, nor have we heard of its ever having spread beyond England. The system of Sol Babitz of California seemed interesting but proved impractical, and nothing more has been heard of it. Pierre Conté's method is clearly limited to ballet. A recent development is the as yet unpublished and unproven notation of Alwin Nikolais.

The one system on which fifty years has been spent and which has proved itself the most practical is that of Rudolf Laban, first published in 1928. The strength of the Laban system lies in its simple logical basis and its universality. In the early stages, any notation system can seem plausible, since simple steps will always be easy to write. It is not until every type of movement has been tried and every rule tested that the weakness or strength of a method is brought out. In the early years of its development the Laban notation, or "Kinetographie," as it was called, was used and spread by many teachers and dancers in different fields. Each person contributed to the notation from his experience and kept it from developing in favor of one particular type of movement or another. Among those who have done notable work in the Laban notation are Albrecht Knust, who has written several ballets of the Munich Opera Company; Sigurd Leeder in England; and in the United States Irma Betz and Irma Bartenieff and the Dance Notation Bureau of New York and its many associate members.

One of the earliest experiments in the Laban script occurred in Germany in 1936 before the staging of a mammoth presentation for a Dance Congress. The thousand dancers who were to take part in the presentation were spread throughout forty different cities, so to each city a dance score of the presentation was sent, to be used for preliminary rehearsals. When the dancers met for the first time, the parts fitted together smoothly and the show was given with only one dress rehearsal.

Since this early beginning the Laban notation has spread as far as Eastern Tibet where recorded Tibetan folk dances are to be found in the History Library at Kanting. Folk dances have also been written in Czechoslovakia, Hungary, etc., and it is hoped that one day all the available ethnologic material will be written in the Laban system, so that it can be studied by everyone.

CONTEMPORARY DANCE SCORES

Within the past two decades we have seen not only the recording of many full-length dance works in the Laban notation, but also the beginning of the practical application of the notation, particularly the reconstruction of dance works through notation. The first reports of a successful revival of a ballet through the notation was from Kurt Jooss, when he taught his ballet *The Green Table* to an entirely new company in Chile and referred constantly to the score, written in 1938. In the past decade he has referred to the manuscripts constantly, particularly when a number of new dancers have joined the company. On his recent visit here Jooss said, "If I ever entertained any doubts as to whether the notation was practical and worthwhile, they have long since been removed. The scores have proved to be invaluable on so many occasions, and have saved time, if only to settle the inevitable disputes among the dancers." In this country the first opportunity to use a score for reference occurred in 1949 when Ballet Theatre was experiencing difficulties in reviving *Billy the Kid*, since so few members of the company remembered the ballet. Zachary Solov, who was in charge of the rehearsals, called upon me for assistance. Though I had not looked at the score since 1943, I was able to reconstruct the needed sections without any trouble.

It was not until the score of the dance sequences in *Kiss Me, Kate* were commissioned in preparation to producing a London company that any real attempt was made to put notation on a functional basis. Apart from the desirability of having the dances faithfully reproduced, there was the additional factor of the easier working conditions and of the time and energy saved. Hanya Holm, choreographer of *Kiss Me, Kate*, was delighted with the results of working with the dance score. Being freed from the anxiety of trying to remember every detail, she was able to devote her time to perfecting the movements and making the few changes necessary due to the augmented company. The usual result of reproducing a Broadway success in London has been that, thanks to the written word, music notation, and drawings, the book, musical score and the costume and set designs have been faithfully reproduced. But not so the dances, for even when the choreographer is there in person many details are forgotten and much new choreography must be done. This is true not only of musicals but of all dance works.

Other dance works which have been written within the past few years are the Balanchine ballets *Symphony in C, Orpheus, Theme and Variations, Bourrée Fantasque*, etc., and in the modern field works by Doris Humphrey and Charles Weidman. There has as yet been no need to use these scores to any extent, other than the few questions raised each season by members of the company. When a ballet has been dropped for several years then there will be a real need to refer to the dance score.

THE BALLET SCORE

The score of a complete ballet consists of two parts: the floor plans and the movement notation.

The Floor Plans. The diagrams of the positions of the dancers on stage are written next to the movement score whenever they are needed. A set of all the floor plans is usually kept separate from the score itself and, since they will be used mainly by the choreographer or dance director, they are written from the spectator's point of view. A glance at the plans will give an idea of the entrances and exits of the dancers, and the over-all movement and formations. They are indispensable whenever any complicated crossing or weaving of individual dancers or groups occur.

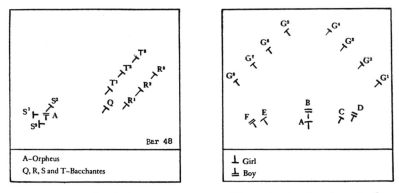

Floor plan for *Orpheus*.   Floor plan for *Symphony in C*.

The Movement Score. The score showing the movement itself is much more complex. Ballet or group dance scores vary according to the number of dancers on stage, and whether they work independently or in groups. A separate staff is needed for each dancer, unless there is unison movement on stage for any length of time. A typical score of a formal classical ballet usually shows the prima ballerina, her partner, two soloists and their partners and the corps de ballet in the background. Thus the score will consist of eight staves joined together on one page, with the music, if desired, placed at the extreme left, the bars of music corresponding with the bars of the dance score.

What factors must be stated in a complete score? Every detail must be stated without which the reader would not automatically perform the movements correctly. The most natural positions and movements are written the most simply. Here are some of the factors which usually must be stated.

A. *The dancer's relation to space:*
   Entrance or starting position on stage.

   Relationship to other dancers.

   Relationship to the audience—which direction the dancer faces. As the movement unfolds these relationships must be re-stated whenever necessary.

B. *The dancer's movement:*
   We must know: the starting position, position of the feet, the arms, head and posture of the body.

When the movement starts we must know: Which foot moves first? What steps are taken? In what direction? In what rhythm? Small or large steps? Is there a leg gesture? What direction, level, rhythm? Is the leg straight or flexed? Is there any movement of the body and arms? Does the body bend? Into what direction? Is there also a twist in the body? Do the arms move fluently, or in a staccato manner? Are they stretched, or bent?

These and other questions must be answered before one can be sure that every necessary detail has been taken care of. We do not realize how many of these factors the eye automatically takes in at a single glance.

RECONSTRUCTING THE SCORE

The question "Are notation scores complicated?" often arises. Dance scores are as complicated or as simple as the ballet itself. Just as an intricate step took the choreographer longer to define and make clear to the dancer, who in turn took longer to learn and perfect the movement, so such a step will take more time to analyze and write, and more time for the reader to reconstruct in the future. This is no fault of the notation itself. In no notation can a complex and unfamiliar movement be written simply. Short cuts, labeling certain movements and steps, will work for those who know the movements, but will fail when memories grow dim or someone unfamiliar with that type of movement or terminology tries to read the manuscript.

This is the problem which has confronted each generation of notators. Are we to have a notation which will be a universal one, suitable to all styles of dancing and types of movement, or is it better to have different notations suited especially to the different needs—ballet, modern, tap, Spanish, Oriental, etc.? A universal notation must be one which is built on the anatomical possibilities of the body, and in which each step or movement is described by the basic elements of which it is made, the part of the body, direction, level, rhythm, etc. Such a notation will make any movement understandable to a person who has thoroughly studied the notation. This is the advantage; that one notation will serve for all, and that a student in China can read a score written in, say, England. The immediate disadvantage is that, since each step is written out fully, the reader must reassemble the symbols into a finished movement again. Whether this process is a facile or a tedious chore depends on the experience and ability of the reader. As with any kind of reading, practice is the necessary requirement to attain fluency. Just as a first attempt at reading words results in disconnected syllables, so the beginning steps in reading dance notation are equally mechanical and unrelated to real movement. The disjointed steps and gestures of the beginner are soon translated into flowing patterns correctly phrased when the relationship between the symbols on the paper and the movements they represent becomes automatically understood.

As with words or music, certain patterns become familiar, and the more experienced reader will read phrases rather than single words or notes. Since most steps are built on basic forms, they become easily recognizable, and it is possible to tell at a glance the general style of the piece. One of the advantages of the block symbols used in Laban notation is that they form patterns easy for the eye to perceive.

It is not so much the ability to learn a notation system, but the ability to analyze movement which is essential to a writer or reader of notation scores. It is because the student must delve into the various realms of movement, into the relationship of the body to space, and the dynamic and rhythmic content of movement, that notation training is of value to any dance student, whether he intends to use the notation himself or not.

THE FILM VERSUS THE NOTATED SCORE AS A RECORD

In recent years the film has often been used as a means to record dance. Some people advocate that the use of movies dispenses with the need to have a work notated, claiming that it is both easier to record and easier to reconstruct dance through motion pictures. These views are noticeably held by people who have never been in a position to compare the advantages and disadvantages of the two methods. It is those few people who have actually revived a ballet through watching a movie, and who have also experienced the use of notation in reconstructing a dance work, who can speak with authority for or against the one method or the other. The situation is clearly comparable to the record of a symphonic work and the printed score of the same piece. To study each individual part, the musician needs the written score. To obtain an idea of the finished work and how it should sound, he turns to the recorded performance. It would be unthinkable to ask an entire orchestra to learn their parts through listening to a record being played again and again. So it is in the dance world. The movie cannot take the place of the dance score, nor vice versa.

THE DANCE FILM

The advantages of a dance film are obvious; what are the disadvantages? The main problem is, of course, the financial one. To make a first-rate movie requires special lighting, a suitable studio, expert cameramen, sound equipment, etc. An inferior work-film can be made during a performance, to be used merely as an aid to the memory. Here we come up against the artistic integrity of the choreographer and also the cameramen. Many photographers will not make an inexpensive film since it is a poor example of their work, detrimental to their reputation. For the same reason choreographers, notably Martha Graham, do not wish to have their work-films shown outside the studio. In order to obtain results that are artistically interesting, certain liberties must be taken and the film will cease to be an accurate record of the original dance.

Among the choreographers who have had experience in reconstructing their works through films are Massine and Balanchine. As a result of his experiences, Balanchine has given up the use of movies as a sole means of recording and has commissioned the Dance Notation Bureau, through Ballet Society, to record all of his works. The results of Massine's experiences are known through the dancers who were involved in the process of watching the film over and over in order to learn their parts. These are the difficulties they experienced: The need to reverse right and left (the movie being shot from the audience's point of view); the problem of analyzing a movement carefully, since slow motion on the screen means the loss of the rhythmic beat; trying to determine the correct rhythm and counts when the film has no sound track; the visual loss of movement through the absence of the third dimension, for instance, when groups cross and dancers are lost from sight; the need to run through the whole film when only a section in the middle is needed. Some of the dancers who quoted these experiences have since worked in the New York City Ballet Company and have been able to see notation put to use. They were amazed at how easily their questions were answered by a quick glance at the notation score.

THE NOTATED SCORE

The obvious disadvantage in the use of dance notation to record a dance work is the scarcity of professional notators and of people who can read notation with ease. These are drawbacks which in time will cease to exist. The advantages of using a notated score have been experienced by only a few, but once experienced they wonder how they ever managed without it in the past. To record the work, the dance notator attends the rehearsals while the work is being choreographed. Whenever possible the score should be written right from the start. As each dancer learns his part and the steps are demonstrated and analyzed, the notator writes them down. Thus the choreographer's original intentions are recorded, not an individual dancer's interpretation. The cost of a notated score is low in comparison with that of a film.

The greatest advantage of notation is in the reconstruction. If there is doubt about an exact rhythm, arm movement, position on stage, it can be looked up in a few seconds. The section of the dance can be turned to, the right page found, the column for the dancer, the measure in question, and finally the part of the body, there being a separate column for each part.

When a ballet must be taught to a completely new cast, the process is similar to the original choreographing of the work, minus the time-consuming experimentations. The dancers are shown where to enter from the floor plans. Then the movement is taught from the actual notation. The notator can easily familiarize himself with any tricky sequences in order to demonstrate them to the dancers. On the other hand, the notator, like the choreographer, can read back and explain to the dancers sequences which he himself is physically unable to perform.

A good example of reconstruction from the score occurred during the rehearsals of *Kiss Me, Kate* in London. In reconstructing the Parade and Street Scene, in which each of the dancers is an individual character with individual patterns, I, being in charge of the rehearsal, proceeded to teach each dancer his part from the score. After each dancer knew the counts of his movements and where to go across the stage, the first attempt was made to run through the entire scene. It was amazing to see the choreography come to life, with only a few mishaps occurring when dancers did not know on which side to pass each other. This was soon straightened out, and the rest of the rehearsal time spent on polishing up details. Had the dancers been able to read the score for themselves each could have received his part, studied it at the same time, and when all were ready the scene could have been put together, thus saving more time. As it was, dancers had to sit by waiting until they had been shown what to do. The day will come when a dancer can take his part home, study it at his own leisure and come back for a group rehearsal needing only polishing and practice in dancing with the ensemble. Musicians do not learn their parts by ear, nor actors their roles by verbal coaching. It is a disgrace that dance still uses these medieval methods.

Thus we see the idea of a workable notation becoming an actuality. We have as yet only isolated instances, but they prove beyond a doubt that notation can and does work. It has still to become more widely used; every dancer should have a working knowledge of notation, and in every company there should be a professional notator on hand to write down the new works.

As a start towards dance literacy, notation is being taught as part of the curriculum at the School of Performing Arts, a vocational high school where students may specialize in dance. Courses in notation are also taught at many of the leading dance studios in New York and in some colleges throughout the country.

We no longer need to prove that the answer to the dancer's and the choreographer's needs exists. We have only to hasten the day when all will benefit from the use of dance notation and the existence of a library of dance scores. In the meantime, future generations will be enriched by a greater source of knowledge of the dance works of this era than of any other in history.

————

Author's note: The Benesh notation Choreology had not been published when this article was written in 1951. The Institute of Choreology in London trains choreologists. The repertory of the Royal Ballet is being recorded in this system, and the scores are being used to teach these dances in various parts of the world.

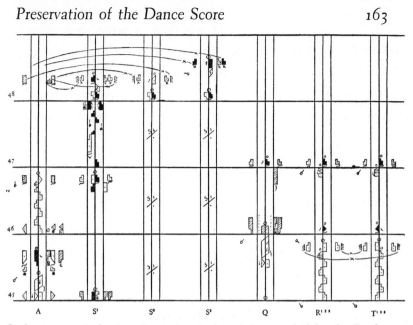

Orpheus to music by Igor Stravinsky. Orpheus being attacked by the Bacchantes. Choreographed by George Balanchine.

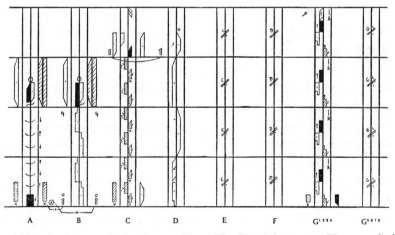

Symphony in C to music by Georges Bizet. The First Movement. Choreographed by George Balanchine.

It is the fate of actors to leave only picture postcards behind them. Every night when the curtain goes down, the beautiful colored canvas is rubbed out. What remains is at best only a wavering, insubstantial phantom—a verbal life on the lips of the living. —VIRGINIA WOOLF

———

JOHN MARTIN

Dance on Film

THERE HAS BEEN a good deal of sprightly talk over the past few years about the affinity that exists between the dance and the movies and the many ways in which they can be made to supplement each other, yet except for the production of a considerable footage of dance sequences by both professional and amateur photographers, virtually nothing has been done to justify all the conversation. The reason may lie somewhat deeper than mere Hollywood indifference, which usually gets the blame; it may indeed be that the natural affinity of the two mediums has been exaggerated. Quite possibly insufficient distinction has been made between the motion picture camera as an instrument and the cinema as an art. The camera per se can render incalculable service to the dance, as the phonograph has rendered incalculable service to music. The cinema art, however, is, even more than the theater, an art of synthesis, and all the individual arts which contribute to it must necessarily sacrifice their own highest potentialities in the interest of the common good. This way we may expect the ultimate emergence of a great cinema art, which is eminently to be desired, but the development of the dance in its own right from this collaboration will obviously be negligible.

The important aspect of the situation, so far as the dance is concerned, is the use of the motion picture film as a simple record of performance. Already Isadora Duncan, Nijinsky, and Argentina have passed from the scene leaving behind them nothing more tangible than influence, memory, legend. By little more than accident a few glimpses of Pavlova exist, an occasional experimental or frankly amateur or obtusely commercial sequence of St. Denis, Graham, Humphrey; but such hit-or-miss trifles inevitably present a warped and pitifully fragmentary picture of any of these artists who have helped to shape an epoch. Though most of them are still alive, active, and creative, already it is too late to salvage their repertoires. Their earlier works have been largely forgotten even by themselves, and the dance has been so long an illiterate art that not even its masterpieces have been written down. It is thus in a position far inferior to that of music; if the phonograph had never been invented, we would lack the interpretations of the Toscaninis but not the symphonies of the Beethovens. With the dance in its present state of neglect, however, lacking the performances of the creators, we lack the creations as well, and the void becomes total.

The need is obvious. The best possible cameras, with the most advanced color, sound, and three-dimensional developments, should be set up immediately before the extant repertory of the great dancers. These recording devices should be in the hands not of cinematographers, eager for angle shots and close-ups but of straightforward technical cameramen willing to set up the necessary equipment and let it operate. The result would have nothing whatever to do with the art of the cinema, but it would be an actual record of the dance.

It is fatal to take a finished dance composition and attempt to make good cinema art out of it. The man who operates the camera must forget that there is such an art and consider himself in exactly the same category as the sound engineer who supervises the recording of music. If that gentleman suddenly became obsessed with the notion of an independent art of recorded sound and began to "doctor up" a Toscanini reading, there would be a general uprising against him. It would definitely be possible for him, to be sure, when the string section of the orchestra is playing an especially interesting melody, to blot out all the other instruments and give it to us unadorned or to cut from a thematic phrase in the first movement to a strongly contrasting one in the third movement and back again or to fade the end of one passage imaginatively into the beginning of the next. Ridiculous as this seems, it is exactly what happens in the vast majority of dance filmings; now we see it from the front, now from the side, again from above; a phrase is clipped here for a few feet of picturesque floating drapery, another is clipped there to show a facial expression or a tense hand or a shapely calf. (The music that accompanies the dance, however, is not so treated; it is allowed, interestingly enough, to play along in full phrase and sequence.) To call any such film a record is absurd; it cannot even be called a dance, since a dance is a formal entity or it is nothing. What we need is records— simple, unadorned, accurate, mechanically efficient records.

That the camera's inherent potentialities can also be fully utilized in their own right in conjunction with the dance goes, of course, without saying. That they have seldom if ever been so used to date is beside the point. A kind of film dance, a chorecinema, is manifestly possible and desirable. The use of slow motion, dissolves, double exposures, and all sorts of distortions impossible in life, could be made supremely exciting. Gene Kelly has already made notable beginnings along these lines within the regular Hollywood channels. But such a medium must be created within the requirements of its own form. Long shots, close-ups, camera angles, and whatnot must be built into the total design in advance. It is impossible to compose a dance in the cutting room.

But not even as a recording device can the camera be accepted without thought. We are frequently told, for example, that the film is the ideal method of preserving dance compositions as well as dance performances, but this theory is open to strong dissent. The ideal method of preserving a dance composition (as distinguished from its performance) would seem to be to write it down in some objective and impersonal method of notation, after the manner in which musical compositions are written. A number of such methods of dance notation have been devised and have proved themselves entirely practical and not insuperably difficult. The camera inevitably records performance rather than composition; specific personal interpretations, the uneven achievement by members of an ensemble of the composer's intention, compromises made by him to conform to these limitations, as well as to others having perhaps to do with financial pressures, all find themselves perpetuated in a filmed dance. There is no guarantee whatever that the composition is presented at its full value.

Certainly there is nobody who would suggest that phonograph recordings could ever replace musical notation. Imagine an orchestra having to learn a symphonic score by listening to a record, with each musician picking out the notes to be played by his particular instrument and memorizing them as they pass! Aside from the forbidding labor involved, this process would make it utterly impossible for any musician ever to study a score and form his independent opinion of its intrinsic qualities; he would be forever imitating (or attempting to get away from imitating) the performance of somebody else. And how, indeed, would the original recording get itself made? The composer, presumably, would carry the whole thing in his head until he got his orchestra together and then teach each part to the players one by one; or, perhaps he would hum to them a general theme and turn the whole thing into a big jam session.

To a large extent both these methods are already in practice among choreographers, for very few of them are capable of composing "on paper." But that is scant justification for declaring them permanent and fundamental practices. It is essentially just as illiterate to dance "by cyc" as to play "by car," and the theory that the film can take the place of written notation is obstructive in the highest degree.

Like almost every other technical invention, then, the camera entails perils as well as benefits, and that is only one more reason why its powers and its scope should be fully and carefully studied. But time is passing, artists are rising and waning; there is need not only for care but for haste.

*T here never was in the world two
opinions alike, no more than two hairs or two grains; the most universal quality is diversity.*   —MICHEL DE MONTAIGNE

BIRGIT CULLBERG

Television Ballet

WHEN FOR THE FIRST TIME I was commissioned to do
a ballet for television, I had hardly seen any television. At once I started to view all sorts of programs and was immediately struck by the shape of the television

---

In dancing and the cinema art the substance is movement, the moving
body and the moving camera seem to be related. Fred Astaire and Gene
Kelly exploited this relationship in the entertainment film successfully.
Jean Cocteau and Maya Deren carried their experimentations into dimensions of unreal reality. But nothing has as yet surpassed the life-
giving spirit of Charlie Chaplin and the imaginative animation of Walt
Disney in wedding movement of the image and of the camera.

The emergence of television created a new medium for the dance. It has
given the choreographer all cinematic advantages and the one great problem of how to make the best use of the cameras within the limited space
of the TV frame. As TV dancing has developed over the years, the dance
adjusted itself to the technological potentialities inherent in the cameras,
and in this marriage of two media, spiritually similar and physically
diametrically opposed to each other, the dance became subservient to
the electronic wonders by submitting to the moving cameras. So far
the TV choreographers have proved the tremendous possibilities that lie
in a harmonious functioning of this marriage approached from this angle.
But now came a rebel and said: "The dance has been abused and violated by the cameras! It will never be a successful marriage until only
one stationary camera will embrace the dancers like a cyclopean eye!"
[Editor's note].

screen. It was rectangular and definitely limited. But neither the shape nor its limitations were very seldom used in an artistic way. The camera was used as a human eye, looking one time at the person talking and then at the one listening, as for motion picture dialogue, with close-ups. We talk about the eye of the camera, but we forget that the human eye is functioning in another way. The living picture seen with our eyes is without a frame and has three dimensions.

True, the television screen is small. However, this accepted shape remains constant, unlike cinema screens. Moreover, the television screen, because of its small size, can spur the artist on to new inventions. It is important to use the whole screen. And it is important to create a feeling of depth and perspective. All this must compensate for the small size and the lack of a three-dimensional effect. The limitation of the instrument often forces the artist to find new solutions which purify his style and make it more expressive. For instance, film was often much more exciting as a silent picture. One was forced to let the picture talk through its symbolic meanings. Before the days of the mobile camera, the actors had to move in a more expressive way. The camera's movements today are often looked upon with more admiration than those of the actor. It moves in close-ups among still figures whose only means of expression is in dialogue.

In the days of the old silent films, it was still a wonder to see people move on the screen. Chaplin was a master in composing almost choreographic scenes where one does not miss the moving camera. One discovers that the movements of the figures on the screen are much more effective when the camera is still.

The old silent films show us that movement of people, things, and animals—riding cowboys or onrushing trains—is much stronger when the camera is fixed. This is quite natural. We see the movement in contrast to something which is stationary. The moving figure is rapidly passing in and out of our field of vision. If the camera is following the galloping rider, then from our point of view, it is the landscape which is moving, and the same thing happens with the camera following a dancer. It is we who are moving, not the dancer.

If you wish to fully appreciate another person's movements, you must remain still. As a spectator of the ballet, you are sitting in the audience, and if the camera wants to give you that experience, it must also be kept still. But how can the small television screen capture the movements of ballet on a large stage?

If we make a ballet for television directly from the stage and the camera shows only part of the entire action which the choreographer has composed, his intentions have already been corrupted and the spectator is deprived of the true picture. Of course, you can place the camera directly in the middle of the audience, but a television or film camera cannot very well shoot the entire stage at one time without producing a very reduced, flattened-out, and uninteresting picture because the third dimension is missing.

One can say, of course, that during a stage performance the spectator's eye cannot cover the entire stage, but focuses his attention on one detail at a time. However, this is not correct, in so far as the visual field of the eye is much larger due to the so-called indirect sight. The television frame takes away our indirect sight and limits the picture inevitably inside its square. When the camera is focused on a foot or a face in a ballet, we have hopelessly lost the total impression and the contact with the rest of the dance. One very often feels that the most interesting action takes place outside the camera angle, and it is even worse when the camera shoots from the side or from above. Here the movement assumes an entirely different shape.

Then, how should one film ballet with a television or a film camera? Let me ask another question. How would you film a stage drama? The question is just as ridiculous. Of course one should not make a film directly from a stage performance nor a ballet. It would not occur to a film director to make a film directly from a stage performance, even if it was arranged for the camera with the same décor. He has to translate it into quite another medium. The dialogue of the drama, the author's voice, creates just as much of an atmosphere as the pictures themselves. In a ballet, the music serves as a complementary auditory perception, but does not provide us with information on what is actually going on outside the television screen. The dancers, not having dialogue, cannot make an impression on us when they are not visible.

As a form of art, ballet is so different. It is dependent upon the space and the visual element. Also, the material is different. The bodies of the dancers are like a sculptor's clay and a painter's lines. A dancer always knows his position in space. He is capable of performing the same movement, on the same spot, and in the same length of time, over and over again. From the mechanical point of view, the camera never had a chance of working with more flexible material. Why not take advantage of these favorable circumstances? Why bother with panning and five or six cameras in different angles? Why not rather move the dancers and not the cameras? It is much simpler and means less time and money than to pursue the dancer with the cameras.

But how are we going to get close-ups of the face? Let the dancer approach the camera and make an artistic intention out of the movement. A close-up makes quite another impression if the audience notices that it comes naturally with a movement forward. Above all, the spectator must sense that it is the choreographer's intention to show the dancer's head only and not his feet. Otherwise, he could easily feel that he is missing some interesting steps. And why not create excitement, making a beautiful choreographic composition, by putting a dancer's head into a lower corner of the screen, leaving the remaining space for the dancers in the background with one shot? By placing the focus between the two and keeping the camera absolutely fixed.

One more very important thing is to tape lines on the floor in colors invisible to the camera so that the dancers know exactly where they are visible and how much of them can be seen. However skillful a cameraman may be, he cannot possibly shoot the foreground and background dancers at the same time if they as well as the camera are moving around. And why all this waste of time when the camera's movements spoil or weaken the movements of the dancers? Keep the camera still, lock it or fix it in place. Draw lines on the floor, even place standing frames of increasing size, if they do not make shadows, and leave it to the choreographer to solve the problems by creating new ballets for television without regard to the stage.

Television creates new choreographic possibilities. The important thing is that the choreographer while creating the ballet sees all the time in his mind the movements through the rectangular frame, and not on a stage floor. The law of gravity can be ignored; the dancer can make his entrances from above or from below the picture. He can show one foot or one hand or suddenly appear as a vision. Superimpositions and floors on different levels also provide new technical possibilities. According to this system, the ballet is composed and rehearsed in a studio with the entire action taking place within a triangular floor space with the camera at its head. In order to have the right angle then, during the rehearsal, it is very important to decide together with the producer which lenses would be suitable for close-ups and total shots at the same time. The camera's distance from the floor also has to be decided before the choreography is undertaken. If its position is at waist height, the proportions turn out well; the legs are not shortened, in which case the dancers appearing in close-ups have to approach the camera kneeling.

This is the way I made my first television ballets. But in the last one, I found another solution to this problem with the close-ups. I had the floor constructed as three different platforms for the dancers to move on. The narrowest section, being in the head of the triangle nearest the camera, was made for close-ups so that the dancers by walking forward could move close to the camera and remain upright. Behind this first section is a higher section which is also wider. The floor of this section is seen at the bottom edge of the television screen, and here the dancers' feet and full-length up to the extended arms and lifts are seen. From this section leading down to the floor behind is a raked platform which widens according to the lines of the triangle, raked only enough so that the dancers' feet are still visible all the time. Finally, the widest section of all is in the background which is the floor itself and is used for group compositions. This arrangement makes it possible to show the soloists to their best advantage on the middle section and occasionally in close-ups in the section nearest the camera.

These constructions allow the camera to be placed quite high without risking a shortening of the legs, and the picture can be large and deep without the dancers covering one another. In this way, soloists in full-length shots and close-ups can appear in front while groups of the *corps de ballet* can dance on the big floor seen from slightly above. The close-up platform is the narrowest, as it is at the head of the triangle; then comes the full-length platform; and finally the broadest one is the long-shot area on the floor, covering the open side of the triangle and ending in a cyclorama.

To save time, it is important to have these platforms already constructed and ready for use in the rehearsal room. With carefully planned and rehearsed choreography inside this triangle, the work in the television studio is shorter and easier because the camera work has been done and only the lighting remains. In this way the choreographer has the hardest job and perhaps also the most interesting.

An important part of the choreographer's work is to make sketches in advance so he can see how his movement ideas will look in the frame of the screen. He must rely on advancing and receding movements in diagonals, rather than movements that are parallel to the screen. He could also use the effect of the big difference in size between the dancers in the foreground and those in the background as well as the strong impact made by rapid movement toward or from the camera. Especially for dramatic ballets, television gives unexpected artistic possibilities.

We can learn from the great masters of pictorial art how they fit characters in movement into the frame. The Renaissance art as well as modern painting creates dynamic tension within the rectangular frame by filling the space with contrasting forms.

The arrangement of these platforms is very practical for ballets with big groups. However, if the choreographer wants to do more intimate scenes with only a few dancers, he could, of course, use an ordinary floor space with a lower camera, but fixed in one place at the head of the triangle. He could also divide the ballet into scenes with different arrangements. But the important thing is that the choreographer had decided the position of the camera for every scene and that this remains exactly the same at the shooting. It is very necessary for the choreographer to collaborate with a producer who understands his artistic intentions and realizes the special character of the dance. He cannot use his traditional television or film technique, but he can put his technical knowledge and ability at the choreographer's disposal.

A good collaboration with the composer is also important. The intimate character of the television screen does not require a great symphonic orchestra. On the contrary, chamber music is very suitable. All sorts of experiments with electronic techniques can give new artistic effects.

The set designer is of little importance in television. An empty cyclorama is the best background because there is not space enough on the little screen and the choreographic lines in the dancers' movements must not be disturbed.

In regard to the arranging of stage ballets for television, my experiences are limited to my own choreography. In these cases, I changed the choreography almost entirely. I deem it necessary in order to create effective television ballet. The same is applicable for all classic works or those whose choreographers are no longer alive. I consider the arrangement with the plat forms on different levels also as a good technical solution for the larger classic works.

This is briefly what I have arrived at as a choreographer for television. It is not my intention to make rules or to present a ready-made solution. It is just one practical suggestion which could be modified and developed further.

Our firmest convictions are apt to be the most suspect, they mark our limitations and our bonds. Life is a petty thing unless it is moved by the indomitable urge to extend its boundaries. Only in proportion as we are desirous of living more do we really live. Obstinately to insist on carrying on within the same familiar horizon betrays weakness and a decline of vital energies. Our horizon is a biological line, a living part of our organism. In times of fullness of life it expands, elastically moving in unison almost with our breathing. When the horizon stiffens it is because it has become fossilized and we are growing old. —JOSÉ ORTEGA Y GASSET

For the ballet to be in the least credible, it is essential to be entirely incredible. —THÉOPHILE GAUTIER

———

KURT SELIGMANN

The Stage Image

THE FUNCTION of the stage designer is to create, through plastic means, a climate favorable to a particular dance. Some choreographers consider settings and costumes a necessary evil—a concession to the public which does not aesthetically appreciate the pure form of the dance, and requires a visual stimulant. Their reluctance holds little inspiration for the stage designer who would like to employ bold means and give full freedom to his imagination.

Other choreographers less bound by misplaced purism accept new ideas enthusiastically. However, the most original costumes and the finest settings, like the best musical score, cannot make up for lack of inventiveness on the part of the choreographer, or of technical skill on the part of the dancer. If music and choreography are bold, then the designer too is enticed to use bold means, and the flight of his imagination is unhindered.

Any dance performance should be an entity. The composer, the choreographer and the designer should collaborate to fuse their work into a perfect alloy.

Such collaboration is difficult. The three artists at work must find a precarious equilibrium in which each enjoys full liberty in his medium, but with the implicit intent of working towards a single aim: the aesthetic unity of the dance performance.

Successful collaboration depends on many more people than the composer, choreographer and designer.

The deepest desire of the producer is a capacity audience, and if successful he will at times give his advice, asked or unasked. He will try to bend the performance to his routine and, because he depends upon the broadest possible appeal, he will be mildly shocked by all that does not immediately please the masses. What producer who is not a Croesus can afford to allow his three artists to experiment freely with complete disregard of popularity and cash receipts? Only a gambler risking his skin would speculate on the new and unknown. Fortunately, those gamblers have not yet died out.

Often a stage technician is assigned to aid the free-lance artist who does not have stage experience. This technician, or scenic artist, may be a valuable help, or involuntarily cause all sorts of obstructions. When working with a painter of repute, his inferiority complex may get the better of him. He may barricade himself behind all kinds of technicalities and create non-existent difficulties.

The lighting technician can also contribute to the success

or failure of a dance performance. Unfortunately, he has little to say. Lighting is perhaps the most neglected of the various departments. The costume designer does not always attend light rehearsals, a reprehensible negligence. And often the decision remains entirely in the hands of the choreographer whose chief concern is the use of light as a means of grouping the dancers or accenting soloists. Light can do a great deal more.

For Hanya Holm's *The Golden Fleece* at the Mansfield Theater a white drop curtain was provided where a black one was needed. The lighting expert was able to remedy this error and produce a fairly dark background by means of his projectors. But he seldom has the opportunity to use his initiative so effectively. As a rule he does what he is told, and too often he is told the wrong thing.

Many hold the curious notion that a minimum of light produces the best theatrical effect. A dark stage makes me sleepy. When it represents the depth of night it may be justified, but then the stage designer must find a way to enliven the stage image. Dim light on drab costumes may rest the eye and the mind but is far from inspiring. I believe that objects and happenings upon the stage should be fully legible. And light is the means par excellence for legibility. If there are enough projectors at the light technician's disposal, he can use successfully even awkward gelatins, dark blues and greens, which are very unbecoming colors. For my part, however, I favor straw and cocoa.

Many excellent designs for costumes and sets look perfect on paper and are works of art in their own right. If the costumes and sets when executed are disappointing, this is usually the fault of the designer, not of the costumer. The costumer often has a strong scenic sense, an understanding based on experience, and can work effectively from a rough and apparently meaningless sketch if it has been well imagined by a stage-conscious artist.

This metamorphosis from costume design to real costume is crucial for the stage designer. If he has not made himself clear, the costumer is compelled to interpret the sketch in his own way, and such interpretation may completely contradict the original intent. The ideal solution is for the stage designer to remain closely in touch with the costumer and use the latter's technical knowledge and familiarity with various materials.

Legibility is the important factor for costumes as it is for lighting. The costume is a fragment of stage architecture seen from a distance. Costly ornaments, intricate details may become completely blurred in the limelight. In *The Four Temperaments* ballet a group of costumes executed in white jersey on red tights were finished with complicated drapings painstakingly done by an excellent costumer. At the opening performance these draperies appeared as quite flat white cloth. The folds had to be accented with black trimming which would have been effective of itself, without the tedious work done previously.

Yet legibility should not to my mind be confused with simplicity. Simple costumes and sets may have an immediate and startling effect on the raising of the curtain. They may be legible at once. But more complicated forms may "wear" better, especially when the performance is rather long. In this case, the spectators' eyes will wander around in a slow reading of the stage image, as of a tapestry whose intricate designs and many colors will never become tedious precisely because of their intricacy. A theatrical mood of mystery may be obtained through fantastic, mysterious forms more adequately perhaps than by means of light effects.

A choreographer will seldom accept uncritically the result of the designer's and costumer's combined efforts. Here a skirt must be taken off and replaced by a tutu, there a wig is too heavy, a sleeve too stiff. Often from the dancers' complaints of discomfort one might think that they were made of eider down rather than flesh and bone. In accepting their proposed changes the designer may strip his costumes of whatever was interesting, amusing or characteristic. Energy and tact are needed to win the battle with a dancer.

Yet there are limits which the designer cannot transgress. Then the dancers' complaints become legitimate. When, for example, headgear or head ornaments are too heavy and considerably restrict the visual field, the dancer's sense of equilibrium may be impaired. Oft-repeated rehearsals alone can remedy this evil.

It is frequently said that the costume should permit every possible movement of the body—an idea all the more dangerous as it is shared by many dance critics. The choreographer argues that the dancer's legs and arms are his organs of expression, as the throat is the organ of the singer. He may protest to the designer, "A singer does not adorn his throat with velvet and tassels. Why should the dancer adorn his legs and arms?" One could reply that not only the arms and legs but the whole body is the dancer's expressive medium. Therefore, if arms and legs ought to be bare, why not perform completely naked?

Dance, of course, has exhibitionistic connotations, and exhibitionism might imply denudation. Where the erotic element should be underlined, nakedness is nefarious. The talent of a Joan Junyer is needed to bring upon the stage girls with bare breasts, or costumes suggesting bare breasts, such as were designed for *The Minotaur*. The cancan can teach us a lot about eroticism. From the music halls it has grown into French folklore and will continue to fascinate the public. The discretion that underlies the eroticism of the cancan has its opposite in the nude dance (*Nackttanz*) so fashionable in the Germany of the 1920s. Serious efforts were made to promote the nude dance, as taught for instance at the Menzendieck school which ultimately failed. Today the nude dance mania has disappeared. But exhibitionism is an important element in any dance performance. The stage designer must remember that the audience identifies itself with the dancers upon the stage, thus partaking in the performance. He must find the means to stimulate this participation. Moral objections are pointless; there is neither moral nor immoral art, but only good or bad art.

"Loose" material, flowing veils may give free scope to every movement, and yet this is not what I would call an ideal solution. They confine costume to the passive role of the "adaptable," whereas, in my opinion, the costume has an *active* function. It should underline, exaggerate, clarify and mystify. There is no need for the costume to permit every possible movement, because the choreographer will not use every possible movement for his composition.

This we learn from the art dancers of various nations. The Balinese elongate their fingernails with metal blades. They are not able to join hands with other dancers; consequently they avoid this gesture in their dances. Certain Japanese No and Kabuki players are harnessed with stiff materials in geometric shapes. Such costumes allow only well defined movements prescribed by tradition, while others are rendered impossible. Actors and dancers of ancient Greece wore buskins, footwear constructed to give them supernatural size, which made them walk majestically and slowly. Why then should our costumes be designed to allow more movements than are necessary for a particular composition? Before starting his work, does a painter prepare an immense canvas which would permit him to execute a painting of any size, even if the result is to be a miniature, an infinitesimal part of this colossal canvas? Is it not more logical to plan a specific size for each art work and make the canvas to measure?

The planning of the costume is a subtle affair, as is every form of artistic collaboration. The designer may surprise the choreographer with costume sketches which appeal to him so much that he wants to build his dance composition upon the designer's costume ideas. Even attitudes of the sketched figurines may give stimulus to the choreographer. On the other hand, the designer may get his inspiration from hearing the musical score or from watching dance rehearsals.

Costumes can express symbolic ideas connected with the dance composition, or carry the spectator further into the realm of the imaginary. It is not necessary for the costume or set to fit the choreographic idea as a glove fits the hand. It can deepen and amplify ideas which the dance composition desires to express. For my costumes I like to use symbols, symbols in the form of real objects, not stylizations; real eggs, candles, cymbals, umbrellas, facsimile hands, dice, daggers and all those objects which startled us when we played lotto in our childhood.

These basic symbols cause a chord to resound in our unconscious; they free the spectator's memories and create a dreamlike mood, an expectation of the marvelous. The shock element properly used brings about displacement or alienation. When placed where they do not belong, objects with or without immediate symbolic meaning may create a poetic mood. Surrealists have made ample use of this means: Dali's *Giraffe Aflame*, Man Ray's *Lips in the Sky*, Duchamp's *Mona Lisa with Mustache*, my own *Guitar with Epaulettes*. Such displacements can be effectively used not only for costumes and sets, but also as choreographic ideas. Would it not be an interesting shock effect for a ballerina executing classic steps to be suddenly attracted by a chalk drawing on the floor and fall into a hopscotch? Or imagine a whole corps de ballet performing in strait jackets!

Blending is in utter contrast to alienation. The current opinion among stage designers is that the costumes should blend, blend with one another as well as with the backdrop. I am strongly against this idea. It induces one to mingle every kind of "tasteful" halftone, sweet grays and brown drabs which are supposed to caress the eye but actually are so saccharine that the satiated pub-

lic is not stimulated by color to participate in the performance. True taste and creativeness speak more bluntly. It is astounding how many straightforward colors and sharp forms the stage can absorb.

I have used bright reds, sharp yellows, blue and purple, etc., in front of a drop painted entirely in gray tones. The brutal separation of gray background and vividly colored costumes did not disrupt the stage image. On the contrary, the tension thus created heightened the audience's awareness of the dance. Other designers have used bright-colored costumes against a very colorful background, as Francés did in Stravinsky's *Renard*. He successfully circumnavigated the danger of the bright costume colors fusing with those of the set into a blurred image completely deadening the dance composition.

There is a further difficulty of which the designer must be aware. He is expected to design costumes as "impersonal" as possible and sets adaptable to various stages. When watching rehearsals he is inclined to adapt his costumes to the physical characteristics of the performers—to "draw" the costumes upon each individual. Dancers are frequently substituted, but not necessarily the costume design. Consequently, to suit the individuality of any dancer the design must remain impersonal. Although this may not be ideal it is necessary. Similarly, since companies tour the country with them, sets must be flexible enough for use on stages of various size.

Such concessions should not prevent the stage designer from producing new ideas. There are many modes of expression and their values depend entirely upon the inventiveness and creative force of the artist.

How *is* *it* *possible* *to* *expect* *that*
mankind *will* *take* *advice,* *when* *they* *will* *not* *so* *much* *as* *take*
warning.   —JONATHAN SWIFT

————

DONALD McKAYLE

The Negro Dancer in Our Time

MUCH HAS BEEN WRITTEN about the Negro in American
dance and yet much more has not been written.
By briefing through the various exciting essays one
can get a vague idea of the historical picture—that is if one can
fathom the fact through the thick interpolation of ingrained
social bias or the even more insidious patina of condescension.
Yet to view the American Negro in dance today outside the
entire social picture is impossible.

Above all, I must speak in terms of immediacy—in the
language of this particular Negro artist functioning in the time
present and perhaps in that way peel away the layers of theory,
conjecture, and patronization and cut through to the bone and
marrow of the situation, the pap on which artists of color exist.

The majority of Negro dancers today fall into the category
of well-trained artists capable of executing the many demands of
their craft. The creative Negro artists in choreography are the
finest to be found regardless of race. This is no accident but is due
in large part to the persistence of yesterday's generations in spite
of tremendous odds and the bitterness of the attainment of only
limited success by some who should by all rights be on the top.

Alongside this young vanguard, we still have the greats of yesterday who made their mark so brilliantly in the only dance area which was open to them—the ethnic forms they created themselves, distilled from the past heritage and emerging in the shape of tap and basic jazz. This is indeed the arena in which so many critics believe the Negro dance should stay and develop as it will, protecting this theory with all kinds of bogus mythology involving such mystiques as natural rhythm and racial physique.

Then there are those Negro artists deeply interested in the beauties of the African past, the promulgation of these little known art forms and the need for the Western world to view them not as a product of savagery but as the flowering of another culture, as another statement of man's civilization, the beauty and riches of his differences.

Of course together with this I must linger on those dancers well trained in the disciplines of Western dance, both classic and modern, who came along before the great surge through, who gave up in desperation or continued in a bitter struggle and are now too far beyond their prime in this art which idealizes youth; or those who never lost faith and had the ability and wisdom to turn to teaching.

I pause to remember how as a young boy I attended my first dance concert with a friend and was electrified by the performance of the young Pearl Primus. From then on dance was for me. Again I think of the many studios I went to after school hours watching the advanced students in class, marveling at their attainment and slowly becoming more and more inextricably involved. I now recall the faces of those students in the ballet classes. There were always a few of brown complexion. Some of them were excellent, some were average, others poor—just like all the other students. From that group of faces many of the white ones can still be seen on the stages of the world with ballet companies. Others have since retired because they were

Pearl Primus, world-famous dancer and choreographer of unequaled emotional intensity, in *Yanvaloo*

Photo by Gjon Mili; courtesy of Pearl Primus

at best *corps de ballet* material and only a soloist can be sustained in a company after he reaches his prime. The only brown faces that can be found from that group on the professional stage are those who had the wisdom and fortitude to leave this country and go to Europe.

I had the fortune of entering into the modern dance because of my personal temperament and approach. Doors opened faster in this arena because modern thought went along with modern method, not because of any physical or emotional proximity to modern dance that the Negro did not possess for ballet. Of course, this was not by any means one hundred percent and along with this I and many of my colleagues struck out for jobs in the commercial theater. The trend was modern. DeMille, Tamiris, Michael Kidd were changing the nature of things on Broadway, and we were well trained to meet the opportunity. But not so fast. Here as in all areas there was a battle to be waged and some two hundred years of education to undo. We had to fight through the union to be allowed to audition and then often go through the ignominy of being dismissed after giving auditions which our fellows applauded—a thing not often done when one is competing for a desired position.

A breakthrough was finally made not without the use of picket lines, such as in the case of *Subways Are For Sleeping*, a play set in New York City, somehow conceived by its producers devoid of its teeming Negro population. Usually the quota established per show was one Negro couple, used judiciously not to attract too much attention. Again the situation through continued persistence has changed and the phenomenon of a truly integrated show on Broadway is now fact. The superbly talented Carmen de Lavallade was actually described by a columnist in a rave mention as a "ravishing brunette." This, when viewed in the irony of its context, was hilariously heralded in the inner circle as a true mark of the status or arrival.

In the concert dance, those white choreographers that used

Negro dancers as artists with no prejudgment because of color were opposed by leading critics of the press. It was perfectly all right for white performers to be orientals, Negroes, or just anything the convention of the work asked for—but for Negroes, unthinkable and lacking in "theatrical verisimilitude." Of course the Negro dancer who lived as a Negro in American society recognized this all too clearly for the sham it was and realized quite adroitly that it was much easier to take the boy out of Kentucky than it was to take Kentucky out of the boy.

One brilliant Negro artist performing in Martha Graham's *Dark Meadow* was told with blank-faced innocence that the beauty of her performance transcended her race. Fortunately she quickly replied that everything she did was a product of her race as well as every other faculty that joined to make her what she was. The same dancer was telephoned by a prominent choreographer to take part in a production for which, as the choreographer stated, she was looking for "professional Negro dancers." Again with surgeonlike precision she answered, "the only professional Negro I know of is Step-and-Fetchit." The choreography that resulted from the above-mentioned incident was of course a sham and no amount of good intention could help it.

In the choreographic field, the Negro artist of today has blazed his own trails. Works of American Negro artists are represented in many companies throughout the world. They are not limited to nor do they necessarily exclude Negro source material. In other words, the Negro as an artist is recognized rather than the artist as a Negro. It is also sadly true that their own country is far behind in realizing this valuable source.

In the commercial theater my own services are sought after by producers and directors of shows with many subject matters, most of which are not so-called "Negro material." The very fact that Negro creators are used for the "Negro show" is an event of significance. Producers are interested in the facts of the situation and no longer want to perpetuate the hand-clapping, I-got-rhythm stereotype so dearly beloved of yesterday. The fact that they realize, the white majority which supports the theater is willing, interested, and demands to see the truth is a gain significant as history in the making.

What are the prognostications for the future? It is important for the Negro artists to get together on such occasions as the World Festival of Negro Art which took place in Senegal in the spring of 1966, to take a good look at each other and themselves, while the world takes a good look at us. Much can be learned from such important events.

As to the future of the Negro artist in American dance, it must be stressed that it cannot be viewed outside the whole seething, shifting social scene. One thing is sure. It will not become stagnant.

Donald McKayle created several dances with strong social comments, speaking with passion for man and his desire for freedom and the realization of his being. *Games*, his first work created in 1950, reflects the joy and terror of poor children in big cities

Photo by Philippe Halsman; courtesy of Donald McKayle

We wholly conquer only what we assimilate.

—ANDRÉ GIDE

———

WALTER TERRY

Favorable Balance of Trade

A CURIOUS PARADOX has been developing ever since the Second World War. Take as example the Nederlands Dans Theatre, which Ted Shawn brought to his Jacob's Pillow Dance Festival. It represented both an import and an export. How is that? Well, it is genuinely a Dutch company, but its codirector, Benjamin Harkarvy, is an American. Furthermore, he choreographs for the company, as do John Butler and Glen Tetley, Americans both.

Whenever the Royal Winnipeg Ballet tours the United States, we see a repertory which includes choreographic works by our own world-famous Agnes de Mille, by the young James Clouser (and by Harkarvy, possibly) performed by a troupe which includes several first-rank dancers who are Americans.

Speaking of Canada, I recall the reversal of a trend: Once, some of the best Canadian dancers left home to join American troupes (the great Melissa Hayden among them); today, the tide has turned as U.S. dancers head northward to dance opportunities in a nation which grants governmental subsidies to its arts.

The incidences I cite are by no means isolated. They are more than a trend. They constitute a surge.

American dancers and choreographers seem to be everywhere around the world. And it was hardly any time ago at all when we had a real inferiority complex about our version of the dance art. The best, we were convinced, had to be imported. And we received precious little encouragement from our ancestral cousins abroad. They let us know rather clearly that our culture, if any, was rough around the edges and that our own dance evolvements—such as modern dance as represented by Martha Graham, Doris Humphrey, José Limón, and others—were too remote from ballet to be given any kind of serious consideration.

True, there were some dazzling exceptions. More than a century ago, a Philadelphia girl, Augusta Maywood, not only triumphed in her homeland but went on to become the first American to dance as a ballerina with the Paris Opéra (then, the world capital of ballet; more recently, a desperately chic dance necropolis). Her colleague, Mary Ann Lee, also from Philadelphia, dashed to Paris right after *Giselle* had its historic *première*, learned it, and brought it back home as a vehicle for herself.

In the 1790s, John Durang, from Philadelphia, a fine ballet artist, had been admired by President Washington, and about a half century later, another Philadelphian, George Washington Smith, handlebar mustaches and all, was selected by Fanny Elssler to be her partner for certain of her appearances on her spectacular American tour. (It would seem that all American dancers come from Philadelphia, or should.)

At the beginning of this century, first Loie Fuller, then Isadora Duncan and Ruth St. Denis made tremendous impacts in Europe, not only in the field of dance but, perhaps, even more so, in theater, music, stagecraft, and, especially, esthetics and philosophy. In the 1920s, Ted Shawn, as a soloist, was given 47 curtain calls in Munich (he was less successful in Cologne—something like 28 bows).

Ethel Winter, one of the most gifted dancers of our time, represents continuity of the expressionistic modern dance in terms
of Graham technique and personal style. A member of the
Martha Graham Company in one of her own dances, *Suite of
Three*

Courtesy of Ethel Winter

But these, as I say, were the remarkable exceptions. We had to tag the word "Russian" on to ballet here—whether it was Russian or not—in order to sell it. Few American dancers went abroad (Ruth Page was one of these few). So we did what we could at home, with our inferiority complex, such as creating an American ballet, exploring and extending modern dance, developing the greatest musical comedy dancing in the world, and, in little studios scattered across the country, learning how to do Spanish, Hindu, African, Afro-Cuban, and other national dances as best we could.

And now we are exporting our dance and our dancers, and the Old World seems to be clamoring for them. In Cologne, where Shawn was briefly, though fervently, cheered, Todd Bolender is now the ballet master, the chief teacher and the principal choreographer at the *Opernhaus*. (Before that, he had staged his ballets for the newly formed Turkish ballet and had done all the choreography for an all-Turkish production of *Kiss Me, Kate!*)

Long before Bolender tackled a Turkish task, other choreographers for American musicals had pioneered abroad. Naturally, in England, American choreographers had long come over to stage their numbers for popular American musicals in London productions. But Mary Anthony went to Italy to do dances for shows and for television. Donald Saddler became a popular favorite—twice he has won the Italian equivalent of the Oscar for his musical comedy dances—and, interestingly, when London imported a successful musical from Rome, the choreographer was Saddler.

Then the floods began. Every light opera house in Europe wanted to do an American musical, and they wanted American choreography to go with it. What triggered it was American jazz or, more broadly, our adaptation of jazz and free movement forms for whatever the subject might be.

Americans were not only hired by the job; they were hired,

at times, as permanent staff members of European theaters with the understanding that they would choreograph musicals and operas plus teaching daily classes in ballet and in jazz.

Bolender has a permanent headquarters, and so do other Americans, but someone like Gene Nettles is almost like an itinerant choreographer-director-teacher-coach, even journeying behind the Iron Curtain to assist national companies in mounting American musicals. Thomas Andrew, choreographer of the New York City Opera, was sent to Warsaw by our State Department to create the dances for multiple productions, in Polish, of *My Fair Lady*.

Europe's monopoly on ballet prestige has also been broken and, incidentally, at the request of Europeans. Not only do choreographers such as Bolender stage ballets as a part of an over-all opera-operetta-musical production schedule but big ballet troupes, not associated with musicals, have asked for and received American ballets. Heading the list, of course, is the Russian-born George Balanchine, whose ballets, generously given, are to be found around the world.

Whether the world thinks of Balanchine as Russian or American, the majority of his creations which he has presented to the Royal Danish Ballet, the Paris Opera Ballet, and many other companies, were created here in America during his residence of more than thirty years.

Jerome Robbins, naturally, is much in demand around the world—indeed, he had had many invitations to stage a new *Les Noces* abroad, but the American Ballet Theatre got it and with it a Robbins masterpiece. But the Royal. Danes, for example, have his ebullient *Fanfare* and have made it their own.

And thus it goes. We are exporting our dance art constantly—even in the ethnic field, one of the truly great Spanish dancers of our day, Maria Alba, is an American—and the strange thing is that when we come to import, in the future, exotic and historic attractions from abroad, we are quite likely to see our own exports coming back to us as imports! Paradoxical it is, but it does represent a true art exchange in dance, no longer one-sided, but now equal. So Ole!, as we say in Brooklyn (well, that's where José Greco hails from).

Late resounds what early sounded.

—GOETHE

————

HELEN TAMIRIS

Present Problems and Possibilities

AVING WON its place in the theater again, where it can reach large masses of people, the dance can only maintain its vitality there by continuing its experimentations, by developing its techniques, by giving performers opportunities to develop their talents. By this I mean enlarging the field of independent dance, dance on its own terms and not only in its collaborative role in the theater.

Perhaps it is significant that whenever an artist chooses to work strictly in his own medium, starting from his own conceptions, such as unasked-for symphonies, easel pictures, or choreographic compositions that are not commissioned, he generally has a hard time finding audiences for these works and consequently an even harder time making ends meet. Because this independent approach is unprofitable, should it be dropped in favor of collaborative efforts? I say no: The artist must be given a chance to develop his unique contribution in whatever medium he operates. Actually the vitality of creative collaboration depends upon the artist's development of his own ideology, his own style and craft. This can only be gained by working on themes that come from him, seem important to him, and are expressed purely through his own medium. He is then better able to give of himself in a collaborative effort and in return is enriched by contact with the other arts. As to the performing artist, he has a better chance to develop his talent because he can work with different choreographers in a variety of roles.

At the moment the ballet field is in a more advantageous position to operate on its own terms. It can find fairly extensive financial support, enabling it to maintain large and small companies, where choreographers and dancers can devote themselves primarily to independent dance works. The modern dance, on the other hand, never has had sufficient patronage to sustain any large company. The economic backbone of whatever small company emerged was the private resources of the individual choreographer around whom the company was formed.

Partisans of either the modern dance or ballet, when speaking of the future of the dance, inevitably see the flowering of only the form to which they are devoted. The truth of the matter is that at this point in history both are finding large audiences. The current vitality of both mediums, in its acceptance by the theater and in the concert field, emerges because each form, within the last twenty years, has learned from the other. The ballet became aware of a wider range of movement, of the potentialities of handling serious themes, and of the fact that America was not an untouchable subject. The modern dance only reached its current wide public by recognizing values it had previously denigrated—such as the use of rich and colorful costumes, the value of spectacle and virtuosity in their proper place—and the technique itself broadened to include vital concepts of movement and line traditionally associated with the ballet. Both have profited from this exchange. Also in the theater field, ballet choreographers cannot avoid the necessity of casting some modern dancers in their shows, and modern choreographers, on the other hand, find it necessary to use some ballet dancers in their companies.

The dance as a whole is riding the crest of popularity today. No musical is complete without a substantial portion devoted to dance. However, this is the time to take stock and see how the dance can consolidate itself, broaden its horizons, for nothing is more vicious than Broadway's craze for novelty. What will we do when the novelty wears off? The only answer is that creative, vital art is always new. Consequently, the real problem is and will always be how to maintain and develop our creative vitality.

In the Forties the commercial Broadway theater discovered the dance and enriched itself with the principles that choreographers have arrived at through years of experimentation. That first fine burst of energy coincided with the avidity for change on the part of the theater-going public. The concept of dance as an integral part of the script, where the dances are used to replace a dramatic or comedic scene, was the main contribution. The songs, too, are choreographed instead of being performed with stereotyped illustrative gestures.

By means of scripts of substance and creative use of dance, the "new" musical was created. It seemed that we would go on exploring and experimenting forever, never to return to the old forms of operetta and the musical show. But the giant steps taken then, slowed down to a walk, albeit a hesitating one. Scripts have become shoddier, diversion for diversion's sake resorted to, absurd dances inserted, the movement vocabulary hackneyed, adding up to a pervasive sense of mediocrity.

But the good fight still remains with some of our writers and producers, and the ensuing years turned up a few productions in the spirit of the Golden Age of the Forties, such as *Plain and Fancy, West Side Story, My Fair Lady,* among others. Now in the early Sixties only *Fiddler on the Roof* has brought some freshness to the dance elements of the script and an overall choreographic continuity and pace. In respect to the latter contribution of over-all "dance-feel," *Hello Dolly* is well served although the movement vocabulary has relied on familiar "steps."

In spite of the retrogression we are now experiencing in the mid-Sixties, the entire world recognizes that the United States has created its own style of musical theater. So much so that we now possess a large repertoire of classics. Some of these have toured abroad as cultural ambassadors, sponsored by the State Department. Interestingly enough in contrast to the professional theater, there has been a continually rising and rich development of dance in the colleges and universities throughout the country.

The original impetus made by the modern dance in the Thirties is still being nurtured and has borne fruit. Institutions of learning now include dance majors offering B.A., B.C., B.E.A., M.A., M.S., and Ph.D. degrees in dance and the related arts. Dance not only has been recognized as a valuable element in education but as an art is no longer foreign to the atmosphere of academe.

Professional choreographers and performers (including those functioning in the classic ballet style) are part of the faculty for specified periods of time as "artists-in-residence." They create new works, often restage pieces out of their repertoire, teach, and lecture. The artist-in-residence provides the student with a variety of attitudes toward dance, running the gamut from the expressionistic-representational to the avant-garde point of view.

The dance workshops provide the productions with dancers who have had several years of daily dance technique scheduled in the curriculum, and the result is a higher level of dance performance. It is also common practice for the student choreographer and performer to give their own programs. Often they are sent out on the college touring circuits in the East, South, Middle West, and Far West. Some perform in the larger cities —testing their choreographic and performing talents against professional standards. Through these developments and the awakened understanding of the performing arts as a part of the

American scene, one can envision the university or college becoming the cultural center of a community.

So far as the "concert field" is concerned, much has taken
place. Here is the matrix—the center and heart of dance as an
art. Its focus on dance as a means of communication projected
through the personal vision of its choreographers, its experiments
in ideas, methods, and movement vocabulary feed and influence
the other fields of musical comedy, dance in education, and
even television.

The Sixties will go down in history as the time when the
foundations and our government became aware of the power of
dance on a large scale. Pressure for such recognition began in
the early Thirties. In great part it took the arrival of the
Moiseyev Dance Company and the Bolshoi here to stir them up.
The phenomenal success of these companies throughout the
country, with their record-breaking audiences, brought home
the propaganda values of these attractions aside from their intrinsic artistic worth.

The New York City Ballet Company became the bene-
ficiary of $6 million awarded by the Ford Foundation to the
amazement and bewilderment of the entire dance world. No
such amount of money had ever been allocated for dance and no
single company had ever been on the receiving end.

Naturally, there was much debate and discussion, both
publicly in the press and privately. So far as the modern dance
was concerned it was left out in the cold. Acknowledged as the
only indigenous style of dance America has created, being ignored
was a great setback, to say the least. Although there was constant
criticism of this large disbursement of funds to the New York
City Ballet and its subsidiaries, there were others who believed
that recognition of even one part of the field would eventually
benefit all. The latter has proved farsighted and correct for there
now seems to be promises of extensive aid to modern dance and
other ballet companies.

Joyce Trisler and James Truitte in *Lester Horton's* masterpiece *The Beloved*, as presented by the Alvin Ailey Company. Horton had a flair for theatrical dance and bold choreographic and visual designs.

Photo by Dominic

It has taken over thirty years—since the first attempt in
1931—at a dance repertory theater in America, that, at that time,
included Martha Graham, Doris Humphrey, Charles Weidman,
and Helen Tamiris, for its seed to take root.* It seems that
several generations of choreographers were needed to plow the
field. In 1964, the American Dance Theater became the natural
heir to the effort of three decades. It was the first modern dance
group that received public subsidy fulfilling the promise of
those pioneering years. But similar to the early attempt when
several companies appeared on the same program in repertory,
the goal still to be achieved in the Sixties is a single company
serving various choreographers and permitting more rehearsal
time for both its choreographers and performers and commis-
sioning of new works of music.

The modern dance has proved itself resilient and in spite of
little or no financial support it is still pioneering. During the
Fifties and up to the present time our modern companies
brought American dance to South America, Europe, and Asia
under the auspices of the State Department. The "cultural ex-
plosion" is erupting all over America, and it is being financed
by foundations, Federal and State Governments. What has been
referred to by some wit as our "edifice complex" has been responsible for compounds like Lincoln Center, mushrooming
over the country. The buildings are going up fast, faster than
the essential planning for what will take place in the buildings.
Let us hope that our cultural advisors in Washington and
elsewhere not only will keep apace with the building boom but
will anticipate it, so that the Performing Arts and our audiences
can be better served.

------

* Helen Tamiris organized this first dance repertory theater. In its
second season with the intention to have more choreographers participate, Helen Tamiris invited Agnes de Mille who joined the group
[Editor's note].

In the main, this has been an optimistic report. I have deliberately closed my ears to the bothersome noises around us: shrill sounds with emphasis on "opportunism!" emanating from the concert field, low growls from college areas discreetly deploring the meager funds for the "liberal arts" compared to the millions for "science," and long moans registered in all keys in the theatrical fields decrying the chase for the holy "buck" that reduces the productions to a new low.

But it is fortunate that one can close one's ears to this abrasive din, for they are, still, sounds of life. However, of what avail "all the plans of mice and men" in face of the loudest sound of all; the omnipresent tick-tocking of time running out, leading us to a holocaust that would put a dead stop to it all?

THE DANCE OF TODAY AND TOMORROW

Merce Cunningham, a former member of the Martha Graham Company, was one of the first to turn against self-expression in the dance. His compositions are an exploration of time and space in a new fashion and create a meaningful world without meaning. Shown in a lyric mood with Carolyn Brown in *Night Wandering*

Photo by Kjell Hedlund; courtesy of Merce Cunningham Company

————

SELMA JEANNE COHEN

Avant–Garde Choreography

THE PAST FIFTEEN YEARS have witnessed the emergence of a new group of choreographers who share the conviction that the proper subject of dance is dancing. They reject the idea that a "story," or even "content" in the traditional sense, is necessary to a dance work. Instead, they assert the independence of dance as pure movement, refusing to make it a handmaiden of drama or music or spectacle. The consequences are an austerity, sparseness, and concentration such as the art has not known heretofore. The new works have evoked a good deal of controversy, with reactions ranging from wild enthusiasm to violent opposition, stirred by the fear that the new choreographers will turn the dancer of the future into a mere robot.

Yet the new choreographers have all had their share of experience in more widely accepted idioms, and many had achieved considerable stature in those idioms before turning to the new approach. Some were active participants in the dramatic phase of the modern dance during the 1930s and 1940s. Katherine Litz came from the Humphrey-Weidman company; Merce Cunningham and Erick Hawkins had danced with Martha Graham; Alwin Nikolais was an associate of Hanya Holm. Paul Taylor was a soloist with the Graham company; Midi Garth and Merle Marsicano had studied at the Graham studio. Not all the avant-garde, however, are allied with the modern dance. James Waring and Aileen Passloff come from the tradition of the ballet. And the best known of all the abstract choreographers (when he chooses to be one) claims sole allegiance to the tradition that developed from the schools of Imperial Russia through the Diaghilev Ballets Russes. He is George Balanchine.

Many of the avant-garde choreographers believe that their innovations began as a reaction to the style of dramatic dance that began to take shape in the late 1920s. They were witnesses to discoveries in movement, the creation of new techniques, which their leaders believed were necessary to the expression of themes heretofore untouched by the art of dance, to the telling communication of deep emotions. The new concept of movement impetus heralded a period rich in movement invention.

The new choreographers have accepted the technical innovations of their immediate predecessors, but have rejected their motivation. While they see that the desire for expression led to the creation of the new vocabulary, they see that continued reliance on expression as the source of movement discovery will limit the growth of that vocabulary. They begin, not with feeling, but with movement itself. These creators are vitally involved in the search for fresh movement ideas. They think of movement as an end in itself.

In extending the scope of his material resources, the choreographer has a congenial co-worker in the composer of *musique concrète and electronic* music. Both have added to the materials of their art, the former by utilizing the natural sounds of the external world, the latter by creating and manipulating mechanically created sounds. Magnetic tape can register more minute distinctions of pitch, more subtle variations of tone, and more precisely timed durations than those possible to any contrivance worked by merely human hands or breath. A similar search had led John Cage to construct his "prepared" piano and Harry Parch as well as Lucia Dlugoszewski to build his own musical instruments. One is reminded also of the modern artist's employment of collage, which has extended his working materials to include so many substances other than paint—wires, newspapers, even articles found in junk heaps.

With such examples before him and without concern for the limitations imposed by either the mandatory elegance of the classic ballet or the expressive motivation of the early modern dance, the new choreographer has set out to extend the dance vocabulary. One way is to seek fresh combinations of movements. Merce Cunningham does this by isolating actions performed by various parts of the body, writing each on a separate slip of paper, and drawing—by means of chance methods—a movement for the head, one for the arms, one for the torso, one for the legs until he has as many movements as he wishes to combine (or as many as the dancer can execute at one time, thus putting a natural limit to the process). More often Cunningham does not carry this method to its technically possible but actually impractical extreme. He has, however, other, equally effective devices. With deliberately composed movements he can still use a chance method to determine their direction and duration. With such manipulation even a quite common movement takes on an extraordinary quality as it is done slower or faster than usual or if it is executed sideward instead of forward as is customary. He has also made notable use of stillness, an element to which he assigns a definite time value and which becomes a positive factor in the choreography.

Katherine Litz shows a similar interest in unusual coordinations, which she calls "inventive movement." By considering each part of the body as an instrument in the orchestra of the whole, she plays one part against another: for example, a quick, small vibrating motion of the foot accompanied by a slow, wide swing of the arm. Miss Litz is also intrigued by subtle variations of movements, perhaps a shift in the direction of the arm from straight center to a point between center and diagonal. Such subtleties, too, are destroyed if the dancer travels while performing them. But since inventive movement is interesting in itself, the choreographer should not need to provide the additional attraction of covering all the stage space.

Miss Litz's interest in the coordinations of inventive movement was stimulated by her association with Sybil Shearer, also a former member of the Humphrey-Weidman company. Having left the New York scene in the 1940s, Miss Shearer has since developed her choreography in another direction (John Martin called her a "nature mystic"), but she did significantly influence the present avant-garde. In the early years of her independent career, she was intensely concerned with the exploration of movement qualities, especially those produced by juxtapositions, of different kinds of movement in different parts of the body. And she, too, felt that this required spatial restriction. Her student Midi Garth shares this interest in movement quality, though she is less involved with its simultaneous complications; she is drawn to movements that are simple yet evocative. Since the basic body pattern need not be intricate, traveling in space may be part of the design.

Alwin Nikolais develops his dance vocabulary by isolating movement from emotional motivation. He defines his method as that of metaphor. By divesting gesture of its familiar function, he obtains a pure movement, a "direct kinetic statement." By carefully watching, for example, the difference in the gesture of an arm that is reaching for a feather and the arm that is reaching for a stone, he abstracts from the movement its qualitative distinctions. These are then freed to be used without reference to any specific context. He defines the resulting kinetic quality in terms of the "primary" emotions (i.e., non-literal, unassociated with any specific object), which include feelings of heavy, light; thick, thin; large, small; fast, slow. They are, he asserts, like sensations of pure color and pure sound.

Still other choreographers have turned to the arts allied with dance for their inspiration in creating movements. Paul Taylor (who was a painter before he was a dancer) thinks of a movement line as he thinks of a painted line—as a direct, pictorial statement or as a wild, shapeless scribble. Thus, a walk, performed in a clearly defined position and occupying a strictly limited area, may suddenly culminate in a burst of vague, nervous arm gestures that seem to be reaching anywhere and everywhere. Either kind of line may be brought into being simply as the sort of design needed to fill a particular space at a particular moment.

Music may also serve as the point of departure, as it does for George Balanchine. The Balanchine ballets that most closely align him with the avant-garde are those created to the music of Arnold Schoenberg, Charles Ives, Igor Stravinsky, and Anton Webern. Such scores have prompted the choreographer to devise movements that diverge sharply from the customary forms of classic technique. They are, however, always related to that technique; frequently they are extensions or inversions of familiar forms so manipulated as to become almost unrecognizable. A man not only may lift his partner (as in a classical *pas de deux*) but may actually place her limbs in a position as if she were a puppet. Routine steps may be done with the knees turned in instead of out; a conventional pose may be shattered by the flexing of a foot usually pointed; a change of tempo or a shift of rhythmic emphasis may completely transform the quality of the movement. Gestures generally associated with emotional involvement—a stamp, a caress—are performed with a cold austerity of attack that betokens detachment—pure and heartless.

Members of the avant-garde are generally partial to unemotional music. Although few of them base their choreography as strictly on the score as does Balanchine, they make special demands of their sound accompaniment. Usually they like it sparse and undistracting. Merce Cunningham, who has worked closely with composer John Cage as well as with *musique concrète*, wants music that cannot be interpreted emotionally. To make certain that there is no subjective influence, he and Cage create independently; not even the basic beat is set, though the collaborators do agree on duration—eighteen minutes of dance requires eighteen minutes of music. Since the composer's method is extremely pliable, often asking of the instrumentalist only that he play as much or as little of a section as he wishes within a flexible time span, the requirement is easily met. But how music and choreography meet at any particular moment is left to chance.

Like Cunningham, Erick Hawkins choreographs his dance in silence. Lucia Dlugoszewski then composes for him a score based on the structure of the "heard pulse," the element which, being common to both the music and the dance, makes neither subordinate to the other. Music governed by melody effects emotional associations that could overwhelm the dance, which is designed to display pure movement devoid of connotations. Because Hawkins is concerned with the dancer's awareness of each movement as it takes place and because he wants his music to buttress that awareness, he cannot let chance decide the coincidence of movement and sound. Sharing a common foundation, composer and choreographer are free to create individual structures without losing their point of contact.

Non-musical sounds have frequently attracted the new choreographer. Alwin Nikolais often employs sounds created on electronic tape because of their complete lack of literal associations. They offer him qualities as pure as those he extracts from his dancers. Sometimes an atmosphere is desired. Paul Taylor has used the sound of rain in a meditative dance for two girls. His *Epic* is performed to time signals ("at the tone, the time will be," etc.), during which the dancer walks, then stands still; walks, then kneels. Midi Garth has done a dance to a metronome which suggested the mechanical nature of the movement, and another to bird calls, to which some of the response was literal, some abstract.

Another element to concern the choreographer is that of the visual devices of the theater. Most avant-garde creators, true to their interest in the self-sufficiency of pure movement, have tended to dress their dancers in simple lines and solid colors (often black) and to give them a bare cyclorama for a setting. But Robert Rauschenberg, the Neo-Dadaist artist, has collaborated with several of them. He has designed a matching backdrop and costumes of points of color on white for Cunningham's *Summerspace*, so that dancers and background merge into a shimmering unity. For Taylor's *Images and Reflections* he made some diaphanous tents that alternately hide and reveal the performer, and a girl's cape lined with grass. Nikolais has made a distinctive contribution to the arts of costume and décor. In fact, he calls his productions dance-theater works of motion, shape, light, and sound. To raise the dancer out of his personal, pedestrian self, Nikolais has experimented with relating him to a larger, environmental orbit. He began with masks to make the dancer identify himself with the creature he appeared to be. He went on to use objects—hoops, poles, capes —which he employed as extensions of the body of the dancer, who moved with them. The depersonalization continued as the dancer was further metamorphosed by the play of lights upon his figure. In each case, the object, the color, even the percussive sounds of the electronic score were designed to become part of the theatrical being of the performer. The dancer who never loosens her hold on a parasol, begins to feel that it is part of herself. Or, clad from head to toe in fabric stretched over a series of hoops, the performer may well lose his sense of self in being a "finial." As the dancer is depersonalized, his accouterments are animized, and the combined elements give birth to a new being. From this being come new movement ideas that utilize dancer and property as a single unit.

Avant-garde choreographers, seeking new forms of continuity for their new vocabulary of movements, let dances take
their form from the experience of creation. According to Katherine Litz, "the becoming, the process of realization, is the
dance." The process stipulates that the choreographer sense the
quality of the initial movement he has discovered and that he
feel the rightness of the quality that is to follow it. The sequence
may involve a sharp contrast: for example, a quiet meditative
sway of the body succeeded by a violent leap; or it may involve
more subtle distinctions, the sway may be gradually minimized
or enlarged, its rhythmic emphasis may be slightly modified, or
it may be transferred to become a movement of only the arms
or the head. Even the least alteration will change the quality.
An exploration of these possible relationships constitutes the
process of creation and thereby gives form to the dance.

The approach to the depiction of the experience of creation
may be analytic, as it is for Miss Litz, or spontaneous, as it is for
Merle Marsicano. She, too, is concerned with "the becoming,
the process of realization," but she does not think in terms of
subtle variations of spatial or temporal patterns. The design is
determined emotionally: "must reach into myself for the spring
that will send me catapulting recklessly into the chaos of event
with which the dance confronts me." Looking back, Miss Marsicano feels that her ideas may have been influenced by those of
Jackson Pollock. At one time she felt impelled to make dances
that "moved all over the stage," much as Pollock's paintings
move violently over the full extent of the canvas. But her conscious need was to break away from constricting patterns of
form, a need to let the experience shape itself.

Midi Garth also believes in subjective continuity that
begins with the feeling engendered by an initial movement. It
may be a free front-back swing of the leg, leading to a sideways
swing of the arm that develops into a turn and the sensation of

taking off from the ground. This became a dance called *Prelude to Flight*. A pervading quality of free lyricism and a building from turns close to the ground toward jumps into the air gives the work its central focus.

Alwin Nikolais objects to art as an outpouring of personal emotion. He seeks to make his dancers more "godlike" by relating them to the impersonal elements of shape, light, color, and sound. If his dancers are sometimes made to look as if they might be creatures from Mars, this is consistent with his intention of placing them in the orbit of another world, a world in which they are freed of their pedestrian identities. It is through the metamorphosed dancer that the germ of form is discovered. In his recognition of his impersonal self the dancer moves, and this self, in the "first revealed stroke of its existence," states the theme from which all else must follow. The theme may be the formation of a shape from which other shapes evolve. It may be a creation to a percussive sound, the following movements, constituting further reactions. It may establish the relation of the figure of the dancer to light and color, in which case changes in the light or color will set off a kaleidoscope of visual designs. Unconcerned with the practical function of his actions, the dancer is engrossed exclusively in their "motional content." Movements unfold freely because they are uninhibited by emotional bias or purposive drive. But the metamorphosis must come first.

Though he is also concerned with freeing dance from pedestrian modes of activity, Merce Cunningham has selected a very different method for achieving his aim. He rejects all subjectively motivated continuity, any line of action related to the concept of cause and effect. He bases his approach on the belief that anything can follow anything. An order can be chanced rather than chosen, and this approach produces an experience that is "free and discovered rather than bound and remembered." Thus, there is freshness not only in the individual movements of the dance but in the shape of their continuity as well. Chance, he finds, enables him to create "a world beyond imagination." He cites with pleasure the comment of a lady, who exclaimed after a concert: "Why, it's extremely interesting. But I would never have thought of it myself."

The sequence of movements in a Cunningham dance is unlike any sequence to be seen in life. At one side of the stage a dancer jumps excitedly; nearby, another sits motionless, while still another is twirling an umbrella. A man and a girl happen to meet; they look straight at the audience, not at each other. He lifts her, puts her down, and walks off, neither pleased nor disturbed, as if nothing had happened. If one dancer slaps another, the victim may do a pirouette, sit down, or offer his assailant a fork and spoon. Events occur without apparent reason. Their consequences are irrelevant—or there are no consequences at all.

Cunningham tries not to cheat the chance method; he adheres to its dictates as faithfully as he can. However, there is always the possibility that chance will make demands the dancers find impossible to execute. Then the choreographer must arbitrate. He must rearrange matters so that two performers do not bump into each other. He must construct transitions so that a dancer who is told to lie prone one second and to leap wildly the next will have some physical preparation for the leap. Such interference is completely legitimate so long as the choreographer does not allow any emotional motivation to affect his decision.

Disassociation of cause and effect is not, however, exclusively dependent on the chance method, and some choreographers have achieved quite complete discontinuity without it. Many have found that reliance on the subconscious and on unpremeditated accident works very well indeed. Some of their productions recall the devices of surrealism; others resemble the canvas set with collage (as do some of Cunningham's, who has

titled one of his pieces *Collage*). One of James Waring's dances
is performed before a wall decorated with a skull, a telephone,
some specimens of type, and a copy of *Time*. The musical accompaniment includes jazz, a bit of Mozart, some rock 'n' roll,
and a few resounding chords on the organ. Aileen Passloff's
Dust uses a ladder, placed in front of the stage and extending
above the proscenium, on which a man sits, slowly turning a
foil-covered box, as the dancers perform their steps completely
oblivious to his presence.

Recent observers have noticed that George Balanchine
seems now to be composing sequences of strangely disassociated
movements. The source of his choreographic continuity, he
insists, is the same as the source of his individual movement-
creation—simply, music. If the musical phrases are spasmodic
and disconnected, then the dance phrases must reflect these
qualities. If the music does not build to a climax, but jerks in
fits and starts to a whimper of a conclusion, how can the dance
build to a scintillating finale? Balanchine has called his *Agon* a
"construction in space" and compared it to an IBM computer.
The idea of the image came from Stravinsky's score. The choreography is as mathematically precise as the music, as abrupt in
its transitions, as clashing in its harmonies. In *Episodes* Balanchine translated the music of Webern into fragmented phrases
of desperate groping. In a strange reversal of a *pas de deux* (that
lovely high point of a ballet, the love duet) two dancers reach
toward one another but fail to make contact; they rush blindly
about the stage; when the man finally comes close to his beloved, he places her upon his back where he cannot even see
her and looks beseechingly out into emptiness. The gesture remains incomplete, isolated from its intended function; the music
stops short without coming to rest in fulfillment.

While some choreographers assert that their works should
not "mean" but "be," others feel that their dances do contain
meanings. In Alwin Nikolais' words, they "let the movement

speak for itself." But it does speak. According to John Martin, Nikolais avoids "dramatization" in the sense of "pouring . . . personal emotion into a merely formal container." Some choreographers decide on an emotion and then find a movement-form to embody it. Nikolais believes that the emotion is not the cause but the product of the movement. The choreographer does not fit the gesture to the feeling; the feeling is already, inherently, there.

The belief in the natural connotations of movement underlies much of the thought of the avant-garde. Paul Taylor justifies his search for new movements by claiming that theirs is the greater connotative power. The balletic vocabulary has lost much of its originally suggestive force through familiarity. The audience looks and says: "Ah, an arabesque!" The pose has become a form so immediately recognizable that their attention is focused almost exclusively on the technique of its execution. The new movement, however, has a significant shock value. Unaware of "what it is," the audience, free of preconceptions, allows its meaning to unfold.

Paul Taylor likes to give his dances curiously vague titles: *Rebus* is one; *Option* and *Meridian* are others. The audience is free to interpret them on any of several levels. Erick Hawkins goes further. His *Here and Now with Watchers* bears sections described as "inside wonder of whales" and "Darling (shouts my body and shouts itself transparent)." He admits that such phrases are bewildering. He wants them to be. After a minute or less of the dance, the spectator realizes that there will be no whales, foregoes trying to pinpoint the meaning, and relaxes, aware only of the immediacy of the pure movement presented to him. Factual titles fill the mind with concepts; fanciful titles empty the mind and let the moving body inhabit it. Some avant-garde titles bear a resemblance to Zen koans.

The new choreographers refuse to be literal. If they can trace their ancestry back to surrealists, who broke the barrier between dream and reality, they find contemporary counterparts in the artists who reveal the multiple ambiguities and shifting meanings of appearances. They draw no sharp distinction between thing and idea, between subject and environment. So in a dance the performer may be at once himself and the forces that shape his personality; he may be himself at this moment and himself as remembered or projected into the future; the dance may depict his everyday life or his dream life or both, alternately or simultaneously. The setting is fixed in neither time nor place. The dancer's stage, like a de Kooning canvas, is a "no-environment," its events detached from the circumscribing effects of particularized surroundings. Any specific clues that could be afforded by décor or costume are eliminated. The performers are dancers, and they proclaim the fact by wearing their professional uniform-leotards and tights. If more elaborately clothed, as they are by Nikolais, their forms belie association with any recognizable period or locale which might delimit their suggestibility. Their faces are usually blank, expressionless.

The spectators are free to interpret as they will, but Balanchine makes an important stipulation: They should come to look at dancing; they should not try to read their personal lives into what they see. All the avant-garde try to keep them from doing so. Let the movement be fresh, the continuity unfamiliar. And the audience will perceive "a world beyond imagination," ambiguous, but fascinating and provocative.

The new choreographer's elimination of emotional motivation has brought about the most serious charge against them, that of dehumanization. "Why," asks one of them, "can't I make a dance about the relation of a straight line and a curved one? You don't ask a painter what his work means; why do you ask me?" One answer is that the painter, like the musician, works with inanimate materials. The dancer is a living being and must be treated as such. The artist should not work against his material but should endeavor to exploit its uniqueness. If he wants to manipulate sounds and colors, he should use sounds and colors, not people.

Vehemently the avant-garde deny the charge. They depersonalize; they do not dehumanize. In the 1940s they found the dance becoming too literal, verging to close to the boundary that distinguishes it from drama. The particularized, realistic character, they feel, is best revealed by speech. The dancer's movement reveals the esssence of humanity; it is evocative rather than representational. This may be abstract in so far as the dance-character is not conceived as an individual; but it makes him symbolic, not inhuman.

Unquestionably the members of the avant-garde have made a significant contribution to the art of dance. They have tremendously broadened the range of the dance vocabulary and revealed its wealth of connotative power. They have explored new relationships between movement and sound, movement and light and color. They have stimulated a fresh awareness of the uniqueness of the medium of dance. If they have not demonstrated that dance must do away with content and narrative or emotional continuity, they have shown that dances can be formed without them. And if their proposed forms are unacceptable, they have at least provoked inquiry into alternate possibilities. Perhaps some of the principles at which they rebel are more deeply rooted in human needs than they believe. But then the shock of their attack may encourage more vigorous direction and growth from those principles in the future.

If some observers cannot yet respond favorably to the works of the avant-garde, the choreographer asks them to be patient. He does not deny the ambiguities of his language; he glories in them. He feels that his contact with his audience is greater than that of his predecessors, for he asks his spectators to join him in the act of creation. Part of the dance, its meaning, is up to them. If they see no more in his works than dancers dancing, he is satisfied. After all, that is what he intended.

> Most artists are sincere and most art
> is bad, and some insincere art (sincerely insincere) can be quite good.
>
> —IGOR STRAVINSKY

———

GEORGE JACKSON

The Living Dolls

IT HAS TRAVELED around the world, but it began in New York in the early Sixties. Then one had to go to a handful of places in Greenwich Village to see a sort of theater, dance theater, that was as new as anything cultural could be. This means that old revolutionaries still can and do point to most of the ingredients as absurd reductions or vulgarizations of things thought up by themselves once upon a time. They fail to find anything but a fad that ought to die momentarily. But it keeps on happening.

On the gym floor below Judson Memorial Church, square-jawed Yvonne Rainer stands like a black-locked Dietrich. With her, like a model for posters of the fair-haired all-American boy, is Steve Paxton. They are dancing in the nude, a simple and sexless little dance. First singly, then in unison. They never touch. Another night they are dressed in street clothes. Paxton unfolds a transparent plastic bag into which he crawls, Rainer, using a vacuum cleaner, inflates it while Paxton balances inside. They deflate it and Paxton crawls out. The entire number takes close to a half hour, for the bag turns out to have been big as a bungalow. Like a faun from an old frieze, Fred Herko pranced onto the stage of the Pocket Theater to take a bath in his own spittle. He scrubbed all of himself and all goes well until cheap perfume is sprayed at the audience at the end of this *Cleanliness Act*. Lean and hungry James Waring, in his street costume—black T-shirt, black Levis, black leather boots—abstractedly wanders through one of his creations, at the Hunter College Playhouse, tearing down an elaborate, expensive prop on stage left and then carefully arranging a casual one stage center, while his dancers are doing an interminable concoction of formal or improvised movements and occasional sounds. In the Brooklyn Academy of Music's smaller auditorium, Aileen Passloff makes a loving parody of ballet exhibitionism with insufficient toe technique of her own but with haunting intensity, oblivious that half her audience has wandered off to the big hall next door (where Caruso sang his last many years ago and where Nureyev recently introduced himself) to see a muscle builders' show. The muscle men can flex each single sinew with amazing control but are surprisingly awkward in total movement, and they lack beauty of soul. So the audience goes back to Passloff.

According to the categories the Living Theater is a company of actors, not dancers. It has won an international reputation with *The Connection*, a Jonsonian comedy about drug addicts. But can one really distinguish between their chance arrangement of prescribed words and movements in *The Marrying Maiden* or their planned Marine Corps drill in *The Brig* and the Brave New World games being played by the boys and girls at Judson Memorial Church? The participants certainly cannot be distinguished by the excellence of their voice or dance techniques. Fred Herko, although he clearly had a considerable amount of ballet skill, and Judith Dunn, obviously a mistress of modern dance, move about on the same stage as John Herbert McDowell and Robert Rauschenberg who are not dancers at all, classical or otherwise. (They are respectively, musician and painter by training.) Judith Malina, the actress, is most likely to be remembered by her high strung way of moving and dancer

Yvonne Rainer by the inflections of her voice. It is not technique
or the lack of it by which this new type of theater is to be
described.

The ingredients of these presentations are diverse. Formal
dance steps from the ballet or ballroom, sometimes from old
moderns, rarely from ethnic sources, are used as freely as the
semiformal movements of marching or playing games, or as the
casual motions of everyday life: walking, dressing, combing
one's hair, scratching an itch, or making love. Costuming varies:
from complete undress to simple tights, leotards, or gym outfits
to street clothes to elaborate costumes and colorful rags. Painted
sets are seldom used. Occasionally stage props are used, and if so
they are from the studios of artists whose constructions seem
indistinguishable from found curios. Vivid lighting is important.
Silence, self-made sounds, recorded noises, or set speeches may
be part of the presentations. If traditional music is played without distortion or addition, it may have as little or as much
bearing on what happens visually as the playing of favorite
records has while doing household chores.

The molds into which these ingredients are poured may be
simple or complex, very short or very long. The simplest are
imitations of actions isolated from everyday life, like Herko's
taking a bath. The most complex are games of chance in which
certain sounds or gestures are cues which correspond to pre-
determined movements, movement sequences, or individual
participants. There are also false cues and part of the fun is
trying to decipher the code. For instance, in one such game
numbers are constantly being called out by the participants. One
soon observes that the number 6 incites all the tall participants
to run and all the short ones to sit down. In another game it
may be an obscure little girl who keeps to one corner who is

the real leader and whose movements give the others their orders. There is seldom a climax. The players simply stop when they get bored with playing, when enough of them have called the number 7 or stamped their feet.

Perhaps a way of describing the new theater is by describing what the audience and participants get out of it. The slumbering feelings of pity and fear that Aristotle felt wakening in him and being purged by *Oedipus?* The surge of pathos and goosepimples Heine got watching *Giselle* with Carlotta Grisi? *Oedipus* can still send us the same way. The sensations Heine describes are to be had today in an obscure corner of the theater, the rare good Dracula film. *Giselle* is put on without horror as a tender and sad little melodrama, a fragant old valentine which most of us go to see not because of itself but because it gives an Alonso, Chauvire, or Fonteyn—at best—the chance to wonderfully pretend or—at worst—the chance to be wonderfully the ballerina.

Plotless ballets, both the old divertissements and the newer models, go a step further. There is no attempt at characterization although the performer may don the guise of a mood or merely the role of "being a dancer." What makes the new (dance) theater significantly new is its dispending with the last disguise. Waring, Passloff, Rainer, Paxton, Herko, and the others are not being or pretending to be characters in a story or personifications of attitudes or even dancers or performers. They are only being themselves. There is, as in no other type of theater I know, the chance for the participant to be naked in his real virtues and vices. Unpremeditated sequences, simplicity of action, repetitiousness and long duration, freedom from the rhythm and form imposed by music are all necessary to help the participants guard against disguises—disguises one so easily assumes not

only on stage. As far as the audience is concerned, the repetitiousness and long duration of some pieces help especially. One is
quickly transported beyond boredom and sees a man, a woman,
men, women being themselves. Why do these people want so
much to be themselves that they practice doing it, in public? One
can only guess at motives and modes of thought. Perhaps it is that
through practice the self becomes simplified; a hostile moralist
might say that it becomes oversimplified and one can no longer
distinguish between beauty and ugliness, good and evil.

The great classical ballets of Petipa and Ivanov have been
compared to courts of law; Fokine's to fine nets; Balanchine's
to games of chess; Martha Graham's to ritual orgies. In so far as
such comparisons help, the metaphysical and psychological traditions of the maxim "know thyself" are suggested by likening
the new theater to Zen psychodrama. But such verbiage probably
does not help any more than mentioning the debts owed to
other artists. The new theater is close to the Happenings of
the plastic artists. But in Happenings, the materials are gathered
and the environment for creation is prepared. The creative
act itself occurs in the mind of the observer and if humans
are used, they are props, not themselves. Chance has been
much explored by Merce Cunningham, but he usually keeps
close to formal, almost balletic movement. Cunningham, col-
laborating with composer John Cage, also uses sound casually
and the whole idea of freedom from music can be traced back
through Roland Petit and David Lichine to Serge Lifar, perhaps even to Petipa. On the other hand, the formal musical
influence of a Balanchine can also be detected. If not within a
piece then in the order of pieces, as on one of the new theater's
best evenings when Yvonne Rainer presented a very long, chance
Games; a very passionate, very dressed, very brief *Love;* and a
final, formal *Bach.* Is there any end to tracing sources? Some
people see the nineteenth century's living pictures as ancestors
to both Happenings and the new theater. Chance games are

called sterile, mechanized heirs of the old improvisations. But arguments about lineage do not define the core.

It does depend on whether one thinks man is fallen and must be saved by pretending or whether one believes that the soul, naked in its native beauty and ugliness, is the most wonderful of all things to see.

*A man lives not only his personal
life, as an individual, but also, consciously or unconsciously, the life
of his epoch and his contemporaries.*   —THOMAS MANN

―――

ALWIN NIKOLAIS

Growth of a Theme

IN THE STRICTEST SENSE of the word I do not believe there is
any such thing as contemporary or modern art. What is
really meant by those words is the contemporary aspect or
vista of art. We would hardly say there is a contemporary moon
or contemporary stars. Yet we might describe the moon as we
see it today—that is, from the vantage point of a contemporary
time.

So it is with art. It is always there, but through change of
historical climate and maneuverings of mankind we find ourselves transported to new revelations of it.

Devices, techniques, methods, and forms are materials
in between art and the artist—attached to neither one, they are
in themselves relatively meaningless. They do not by themselves
constitute art or modernism. Modernism is not a method. It is
fundamentally a state of mind, a vantage point from which one
sees his world.

One of the major characteristics of our current dynamics is
our capacity to transcend the literal and to replace it with an
abstract metaphoric language.

The dance artist, when he composes, can subdue his literal
character and invite attention to the motion, the shapes, and to

the time and space in which these occur. He has found means to make a direct language of motion and to use his literal figure as a sensitive instrument to enact delicately the drama of motion.

Each new perspective of art breaks down another barrier in man's quest for freedom. The major characteristic of the contemporary vista of dance is freedom. But it is freedom in bondage to the subterranean and primordial poetry of life which permeates all and everything—that which we call Art.

MASKS, PROPS, AND MOBILES (1954)

This original effort was toward transcendence—transcending a central emotional state of dancing into a more heroic figure by use of masks or props—thus creating of the dancer an archetype rather than a pedestrian emotional figure.

In the section called "Web," the dancer was involved in an entire stage of motion rather than in a motional or emotional state with other dancers. The linear designs controlled by the dancers in space were to me as important as the dancer's own figure in motion.

In the dance "Noumenom" the idea of masking for the purpose of enlarging was now extended over the whole body. Out of this grew a totally non-literal, non-objective dance. Here the dancer brought to life free-formed sculptural shapes without revealing his own physical body. "Noumenom" reveals a close kinship with contemporary art emphasis. Reflections of this non-literal area of abstraction are visible in later dances. [Parts of "Noumenom" were filmed for the Ford Foundation series of educational TV films *A Time To Dance*.]

Similar methods produced "Tournament," in which the sculptural manipulations of a cape became the essential dance design. This dance later became the finale of my first evening-long work, *Kaleidoscope*, which was the result of further exploration of the idea of the archetype.

Vaudeville of Elements (1966) shows *Alwin Nikolais* taking
another exploratory step into the world of his total theater of
movement, sound, color, and light

Photo by Susan Schiff Fuladi courtesy of Henry Street Playhouse

KALEIDOSCOPE (1955)

The dancer was neither dehumanized nor depersonalized; he was elevated to a plane someplace between common man and divinity. *Kaleidoscope* further introduced the use of props or other means of extending the body as an abstract protagonist. The dances were titled after the extensions with which they were involved: "Discs," "Pole," "Paddles," "Skirts," "Bird," "Hoop," "Straps," "Capes." The relationship of dancer and prop became the dramatic *raison d'être* of each episode. The dancer was part of a totally designed stage in which the painting of the face, hands, and feet continued the design of the costume into a total figure. In *Kaleidoscope*, too, there was introduced the idea that a program could be a collage of several pieces, no one of which itself had literal significance, but which produced by their summation a sense of a total happening. [*Kaleidoscope* was televised by the Canadian Broadcasting Company, October, 1960.]

PRISM (1956)

Just as props were the conditioning element in *Kaleidoscope*, light was the qualifying factor in *Prism*. The nature of light as it struck the dancer's figure in motion was consciously choreographed. Parts of bodies appeared and disappeared, creating a sense of prismatic illusions. In trying to avoid literal anticipation in the minds of the audience, sections were titled with made-up words—such as "Glymistry," "Lythic," "Paratint," "Tridem," "Prodomin," "Viagrin." Exploration of light factors also brought about the discovery of new time and space illusions, notably in two dances, "Tridem" and "Finale." In "Finale," the dancers, leaping from the back wall, seemingly broke the barriers of time and space. Although I had already done percussion scores for earlier dances and had composed tape music for some sections of *Kaleidoscope* and other dances, I composed the entire tape score of *Prism* in the nature of *musique concrète*. The idea of a palimpsest form was used as an accumulative drama even more strongly in *Prism* than in *Kaleidoscope*. [The electronic scores used in this ballet have been recognized for their musical value, and, along with later pieces, have been played on radio and in concert.]

CANTOS (1958)

Now props were eliminated in order to further explore the abstract use of the human figure as a sculptural form in motion. The only exception was the section called "Runic Canto," with twenty-two dancers, in which props were used to effect a primal cabalistic ritual.

MIRRORS (1958)

This program was entirely improvised by my company of dancers, whose skill in improvisation had now been developed over a number of years. The costumes, lights, and music, however, were predesigned. The dancer, in the atmosphere of this setting, freely invented at the moment, out of whatever impulsions the time and place created.

ALLEGORY (1959)

All elements previously treated in isolation were now merged—the interrelation of dancer, shape, light, color, sound. And it was in *Allegory*, perhaps, that a new realization of abstract dance theater took place. [Numerous color photos of *Allegory* were used by the State Department in an issue of its magazine *America Illustrated* which is distributed throughout Eastern Europe. It was with the section called "Finials" that Nikolais and his company were introduced to the TV audience.]

TOTEM (1960)

Unlike the works that precede it, *Totem* pursued a single subject, that of mysticism, fetish, and fanaticism. It continues in the vein of abstract theater, but it is still too new, and I am too close to it to be able to evaluate what specific developments may have occurred.

After *Allegory* I began to confine my theater works to a single subject. Not that *Kaleidoscope, Prism,* or *Allegory* were without subject, but their subject was more illusive and in a vein of fantasy and non-verbal definition. Their coherence rested somewhat in the style and manner of creation, but I had a strong albeit non-verbal sense of their unity. However, with *Totem* I was concerned with a specific subject—the idea of shapes, motion, color, light, and sound as ceremonies, fetishes, and mystical rites. Yet I did not design any of the sections as specific ceremonies or rites. They were abstractions and essences of such events. I felt I could go on endlessly and I expect to return to the subject, but from a different point of view.

Imago continued my interest in total theater. It was an assembly of scenes representing impressions and activities in a small imaginary village as seen through the eyes of a child. But again, these were not specific, but very free in their abstract evolvement.

Sanctum is concerned with the various shapes, devices, and ideas suggesting place, thing, state of mind, or any situation in which sanctuary is possible.

Perhaps I should say at this point that I begin thoughts on a new theater piece almost a year before I start actual work. I place the subject in mind and let it go to work in sort of an aesthetic "Rorschach" associative process without resorting to conscious intellectualization or reason. When I start work I do so quickly and let the whole accumulation of assembled thoughts pour out. I accept, in sheer faith in myself, that whatever comes is relative to the subject and is to my mind a significant facet to it. I do not verbalize about it nor consciously question it for meaning. When the material is almost fully composed, then I order its sequence and for the first time evaluate its evolution and totality.

Galaxy centers on the idea of orbit—the hanging together of things by their affinities, their attractions, and even their essential repulsions. Here were the affinities of lights and colors or shapes metaphorically and abstractly representing the multitudinous unions which create all forms, states, situations, or identifications from microcosm to macrocosm.

But in asking an artist to describe his process and reason one must expect much to be rationalized and much to be left out. The major value of an art rests in its non-verbal dimension. I cannot propose suddenly to expose to myself the reason and sense of that which I do which relies so much upon felt rather than intellectual reasoning. I cannot describe this any more than a composer can describe his symphony. I must leave that for others to do.

Although I am sure that I used devices of Theater of the Absurd as far back as 1953 I did not do so consciously. Abstract Expressionism, Theater of the Absurd, Dada, Pop and Op art were all tools to my theater—but never consciously. I used them as they served me. I never served them. Nor did I *experiment* in the general sense of the word. Perhaps I did somewhat in 1953, 1954, and 1955, but with *Kaleidoscope* (1955) and after, the works were created directly with no more experiment than goes on in any other form of creation.

The canons of art are merely the expression in specialized forms of the requirements for depth of experience.
—ALFRED NORTH WHITEHEAD

––––––

MERLE MARSICANO

Thoughts on Dance

BY THE VERY NATURE of the dance, as differentiated from any of the plastic arts, each performance recapitulates the act of creation. The concept is alive and working and confronts one as a living presence.

The dance itself, even though thoroughly fabricated and perhaps because it is so willed a creation, confronts one as the living thing, with the mental concept and the vibrant actuality merged into one image. How could we say what living thing the dance symbolizes?

I execute concrete gesture, but is it real? It may be realistic. But the sequence is of a strange order within a world of my own and excites anticipation of its consequence.

I want to find movement of a simple power—perhaps to remove myself as I dance to a time remote and discover the memory of moving for the first time.

The duration of a dance is so short. Upon this pinpoint of time, this three to five minutes of a lifetime, one must invoke one's entire being.

Time in the theater is reflective. In a play there are thousands of words which echo manifold thoughts, and the play of thoughtful speech forms the delightful time of the theater.

The dance is mute. Consider that when I dance I am suddenly bereft of speech, caught, as in a dream, in the fatality of my action. Time is thick and heavy suffused with the portent and urgency we know only in dreams. It is charged and fraught with suggestion.

In this strange interval, in this curious time of the dance, familiar movement may be invested with a new temporal reality. The long reach of an arm can reveal avenues of eternity; the turn of a head can mirror echoes upon echoes of recollection. The dancer controls time. The dancer really creates the movements which contain the image of time. Time can be prolonged, it can be arrested and then re-formed.

Discovery can be prolonged through the elasticity of a dance's duration, as though the time of occurrence were stretched taut. The spectacle emerges through layers of darkness gradually peeling away.

Within the action, the participation of the spectator varies in converging perspectives, as though he were not fixed in one formal position, but made to move as the dancer wills him into the action. I choose the angle from which movement is perceived. The event directly seen meets the eye at a bias of vision, sometimes from behind itself. Remaining purely in a façade relationship does not sufficiently fulfill remote areas of experience that I wish to convey. We enter the room of experience through new doors.

The speed of the event, like the line of perception, is another artifice. I fall and plummet helplessly along the course of movement. Or I move, too, with a torpid reluctance to stir, so slowly that there is time to look at myself in motion. However slow or fast, there is tension in the enchainment of movements, and it does not slacken with the tempo. It is rather like stepping onto a tightrope over an abyss each time I begin to dance. It takes a resistance to overcome the feeling of sailing across sheer, open space. I must reach into myself for the spring that will send me catapulting recklessly into the chaos of events with which the dance confronts me.

The contour of the figure cannot remain within the confinement of its silhouette. The inner contour becomes its outer expansion and establishes its own external profile. Whatever it suggests is placed outside the reach of human extension so that nature cannot reclaim it. It is an imaginary projection into the abstract.

The perpendicular definition of the area in which I work consists of the floor and the highest point to which I can jump. Jumping and rolling on the floor do not particularly suit my mode of expression. I am less interested in hurtling myself at the extremities of space than I am in moving, faster or slower, within the infinite gradations of this vertical extension.

I might want to return from a point in space more slowly than my progress toward it—slower than the return of a jump would allow—perhaps thus implying greater distance and further limits than those imposed by physics or a concept of reality outside the dance.

As for the floor, I want to dissolve the floor. I might put the floor above me, behind me, or at either side. Sometimes I feel that I am descending below the level of the floor, and at times I feel it suspended in strata above me. The feel of the floor, its primary attraction, need not occur under my feet alone. The space about me, as I will it to do so, can possess the same tangible resistance. The experience of my feet as they press against the weight of the floor can be transferred to my hands as they push against space. My hands then become the feet.

I want my movements to ignite the space about me. Within the duration of a dance, it is possible to evoke changing aspects of space and to play with their identities. The air around me seems to have the capacity to solidify or melt. It can be heavy, then rarified, or agitated and then becalmed. Sometimes I have to force my way through it, and at other times I am driven by it.

I have danced to music and have been danced by music. I think of music as an art of untouched white upon which I must breathe for my very existence, yet leave untouched, just as the music must pass through and around me without discoloring the white of my being.

Personality in dance combines identity and environment, and that is its marvelous ambiguity. The dancing figure is the person and becomes in the next moment, the wind. Arrest the dancer anywhere on stage—his condition is flux. In stillness I change. And the composed shape of my figure suddenly explodes in a riot of configuration. My person is a protean being.

> When the Ten Thousand things are viewed in their oneness, we return to the Origin and remain where we have always been. —SEN T'SEN

———

ERICK HAWKINS

What Is the Most Beautiful Dance?

DANCE that is violent clarity.
Dance that is effortless.
Dance that can at all times reveal a tender breastbone.
Dance that lets itself happen.
Dance that dedicatedly loves the pure fact of movement.
Dance that knows the most beautiful and true movement starts in the pelvis and spine and flows into the tassel-like legs, arms and head.
Dance that uses technique that is an organic whole, not a grab-bag of eclecticism.
Dance which does not stay in the mind, even the avant-garde mind.
Dance that senses itself instant-by-instant like the prick of a pin.
Dance that senses itself instant-by-instant.
Dance that loves gravity rather than fights gravity.
Dance that hangs and falls rather than fights.
Dance that has reached such a height of subtlety it can stand still.
Dance that loves time, time as a SENSED duration, and all the subtle asymmetrical divisions of time, and yet ALWAYS the pulse of time.

Dance that never ignores, either audience, or music, or stage, or fellow-dancers. Therefore no frozen faces.

Dance that does not try to explode the same bubble twice. Neo-Dadaism being exactly that: the already exploded bubble.

Dance that is not a sheer shambles and general mess, a new IWW, anything goes, throw it together, kid stuff.

Dance that is grownup, composed by post-adolescents for post-adolescents.

Dance that knows soundness in psyche and body always produces rhythmical movement; that spastic- and catatonic-like movement is illness.

Dance that knows movement and music put together without a common pulse is two people talking at you at the same time. Something is ignored!

Dance that knows you must have live musicians as well as live dancers or you have dead music and dead theater.

Dance that knows that the longer records are used, the longer it will take us to find the correct music for dance.

Dance that is aware of what a woman is and what a man is.

Dance that knows how to show that the love of man and woman is neither soupy nor a misery.

Dance that reveals the dance AND the dancer.

Dance that knows that the art is more than the personality of the dancer.

Dance that uses virtuosity only in the service of "poetry," not as acrobatics misconceived as art.

Dance that does not separate sacred and profane.

Dance that knows dance is a metaphor of existence.

Dance that can paraphrase the ancient Hindu saying: "Let those who dance here, dance Him."

Dance that knows dance can be, should be, and is a way of saying now.

Yvonne Rainer in *Parts of Some Sextets,* one of her dances, in which the creative action on stage seems to be more important than the artistic result of the creative process. She is one of the most gifted dancers of the Judson Memorial group

Photo by Al Giese; courtesy of Yvonne Rainer

> *Experience is not what happens to a*
> *man. It is what a man does with what happens to him.*
>
> —ALDOUS HUXLEY

———

YVONNE RAINER

The Dwarf Syndrome

AT THIS MOMENT of my dance life I don't want to make a manifesto. I feel no more willing to say what dance is or ought to be than the dwarf lady I saw on the street today.

Dance is dwarf. Dance is the Supreme Dwarf Lady. Dance is the dwarf lady of some of us.

But a body of work gives the lie to generalizations. It is the incontestable proof of Attitude. And that's what I have: a Body of Work which might be said to contain the Attitude that dwarf lady movement is O.K. ("acceptable dance content") so long as it is placed in a formal structure and is circumscribed by formal concerns—space, duration, sequence, simultaneity, etc., of sufficient quantity or quality or both to divest it of its anecdotal possibilities.

The above statement is obsolete, referring as it does to the bulk of my work, but not to the most recent bulk. The latest is: Dwarf lady movement is N.G. ("unacceptable dance content"). Its connotative attributes can never be overcome and are ultimately uninteresting and unessential.

So let's get on with some more movement invention.

*The artist is like Sunday's child—he
alone sees spirits. But after he has told of their appearing to him,
everybody sees them.* —GOETHE

————

WALTER SORELL

In Defense of the Future

MAN has made many discoveries about himself in our age and has paid the price artistically. The groping for new forms and ways of expression started as early as the turn of the century and has not yet subsided.

After each cataclysmic step mankind has taken, we were thrown into a new phase of other isms. While penetrating our subliminal being we have discovered our spiritual isolation. While trying to cope with and stem the avalanche of crumbling values since the First World War, we escaped into a variety of outcries and protests, stammering dada; howling expressionistically; embracing dissonance and the archaic; floating with an incongruous grin and a bleeding unconscious into a surrealist world; resignedly acknowledging the fact that we and things in general exist and that is all there is to this absurd business called life; not giving a damn in beatnik fashion, or shouting like an angry young world that we don't want to be punished for the follies of our fathers; or denying dignity to any creative expression by parodying meaningfulness of meaning in so-called "Happenings" which may be anything or nothing and mostly are a spontaneous sputum thrown up by a creative combustion between chaos, despair, and hollowness.

We have come a long way. We have played with chance and "celebrated unfixity," to speak with John Cage. We are so puzzled about what and where we are that we are speechless and extol it in an ecstasy of silence which we interrupt only to make it sound and move so that we can call this Bedlam of Babel modern art. Man has been caught in paroxysms of negation and, since he cannot get out of them, joyfully wallows in its interpretations. Finally, we can *write* the non-book which appeals to the visual infantile mind. The *nouvelle vague* has become the vogue for the novelist, we had better say antinovelist, who is out to glorify the notion that there is no meaning or profundity in objects per se, and that therefore the heroes' passions need not penetrate the depth of the existing vacuum. We have the non-film in form of a stark surrealism shot through with improvisational obscurity.

When Ionesco, spokesman of the Theatre of the Absurd, said that he writes plays because he hates the theater he has revealed to us the dilemma of modern man in disguise of the artist. As an aside he explains himself:

> I have never been able to get used to existence, to that of the world, or of others, and certainly not to my own. I am continually finding forms emptying themselves of their content; reality is unreal; words are but sounds devoid of meaning; houses, the sky are façades to nothing . . . I contemplate myself assailed by an incomprehensible suffering, by nameless regrets, pointless remorse, by a sort of love, a sort of hate, a semblance of joy, by a strange pity (for what? for whom?).

Do we not see many *modern* modern dancers translate these words into their work?

Bertolt Brecht is out to shock us into awareness. He is the high priest of alienating actor and his action from the audience and to teach the actor to detach himself from his own material. We find all this in the modern dancer, too.

The cult of the anticliché has become the cliché of our

Sophie Maslow, an exciting choreographic talent has contributed
some of the more significant works in the modern dance field.
Poem to Duke Ellington's jazz and Lawrence Ferlinghetti's
verses is one of the strong indictments of our time
Photo by Irwin M. Schor; courtesy of Sophie Maslow

time. To express on the stage non-communicativeness has become the ne plus ultra of theatricality. Ibsen, in his ire against all tepid, mediocre, middle-class conventionalisms, had his iconoclast Brand shout: "We go back to go on!" A sophisticated mind, Jean Cocteau, found solace in the dictum: "My discipline consists of in not letting myself be enslaved by obsolete formulae." Between these two notions, every serious artist struggles to find a way to himself and from himself to his time. But how many are there? And in this jazzed-up race of "being different at any cost," how can we, standing in the midst of this jumble of contemporariness and up-to-dateness, separate the bandwagon opportunist from the one who cannot help being different? Particularly in a period of transition in which reorientation and re-evaluation have become the tenets of the time.

Ben Shahn said about this new ism or "ahead of ism" that "when such work becomes dated, its emptiness emerges, for nothing is so hard to look at as the stylish, out of style." True, fads go out of fashion and fashions fade out. But there is a recurrence of style. What the ultra-modern dancer offers today is often little more than what the despair of the 1920s dictated. Protest, the psychic propeller of most of what happens in the name of art, remains an empty gesture when not followed by a creative impulse reaching out from the ur-personal to universal meaning. There is little difference between Théophile Gautier's gesture in putting on a red velvet waistcoat to spite the bourgeois' sense of smugness and a dancer's defiance by appearing in the nude. Nudity is nothing new. In the Twenties, it was as current as the inflation in Europe, and in this country Helen Tamiris experimented with it a generation ago while fighting for her right to express herself: "A new civilization always creates new forms in art. . . . We must not forget the age we live in. . . . There are no general rules. Each original work of art creates its own code."

We can readily see that there is nothing new under the sun. The Dance of the Absurd—like its theatrical counterpart—was begun by Cocteau and his *Parade* in 1917. He then anticipated our growing dilemma—sociologically, philosophically, and artistically—by doing on stage what we are still doing: trying to wed the banality (now mostly spelled *futility*) of existence with the undying dream of man (read *poetry*). The Dance of the Absurd is a dash of dadaism mixed with a spoonful of surrealism, liberally seasoned with the explosive power of expressionism, thoroughly mixed, and then filtered through with double the amount of existentialism. So much that has been done in the theater, in the dance and the play, during the Fifties and Sixties, is only a more resigned expression of the more frantic desperation of man who is about to demolish his past while fearing the future. That, under these circumstances, the result is, more often than not, a non-statement or the creative attempt at a non-creative expression is understandable.

Would then non-form be the new art form of the mid-century and the decades to come? But non-form is negating the basic principles of any artistic creation. How can anything negative—often extended to the point of nausea—be more than a fleeting and chaotic feeling? The greatest art has always been created by immaculate craftsmen in hours of spiritual intoxication and the ordeal of hard work, by men possessed by the fever of forming and shaping, of giving their inner visions the content and contours of an artistic realization. They, too, have searched for new ways of expression time and again. Van Gogh's colors or Frank Lloyd Wright's forms or Isadora Duncan's liberated gesture or Martha Graham's angularity may have seemed explosive, but were not destructive. They went against the taste of their time, not against the taste of art itself.

For quite some time now we have been frightened into the acceptance of the sophistication of the antisophisticated, of the glorification of the banal; of pop and op and other pretenses of artists to have found the visualization of what best expresses our time. The new avant-garde has embraced the flotsam and jetsam of reality and obscured all criteria of where real art begins and the artificial reality—which we have apparently come to live— ends. One is almost afraid to call a spade a spade because it could easily turn out to be a real spade which the artist might present as a work of art.

There is no difference between an eighty-four-inch club sandwich of sliced car grille, billboard faces, and boiled spaghetti, as exhibited in a museum, and a dance *creation* in which the performers play ball as if in a gym for twenty or more minutes only to numb the audience into accepting a love duet which follows it with the illogic of real life, blending the most absurd of Ionesco with the sexiest of the Kama-Sutra and Brecht's detachment theory thrown in for good measure. And, are we supposed to take it as a comment upon our time when a dancer excels himself in static positions sparingly interrupted by frantic attempts at movement? Is it a touch of irony or an elating inspiration when two dancers carry radios which, for the purpose of accompaniment, are tuned to a certain wave length that, one night, may let you hear Mozart, and on another, a news broadcast? Must the art thus become a hoax to the score of the flushing sound effects of a water closet?

Let us give these artists the benefit of all doubts. One would still have to say: In order to create the feeling of forlornness it does not suffice to stand there and stare at the audience while being enslaved by the willfulness of a gadget; and the image of a non-phrase, of barren poses, or mocking gestures will never reveal the chill of life in a vacuum.

The aberrations of our feelings and the perversions of our minds ought to have run their postwar course in the 1960s. Having reached the extreme of negation, the pendulum cannot help but swing back. We do not expect it to return to any former normalcy—whatever that may be. But out of its own ferment a new dance image must crystallize, an image which will not hide its past experience, the artistic battle scars from its struggle with itself during a trying period of chaotic search for its own identity, nor will it be able to conceal that its stamp of a new today will already show between its lines the core of a new rebellion.

Above all, we must recognize that even non-communicativeness when finding its proper stage image communicates. Moreover, there is no denying that a human being on the stage has a human shape and evokes a human response. In short, we will have to bow again to the innate power of the theater, with its limitations in time and space, and admit that emotions cannot be renounced. Emotive forces do not need to exclude meaningfulness as little as they need to plunge into soul-searching pathos. They may even appear on the stage in many a disguise and involve the audience by implication on the remotest experience level.

But involved must I be. I am questioning and searching. I am a desperate human being stranded in the 1960s, in a frightening and elating, a portentous and potent era. I have swallowed with all vitamins and slogans, the realization that I am alone and lost. Now I have become sick of being told and shown all the time that I live in a sick world. I am aware of it. I want to help and be helped. And if I must go through the experience of existence artistically, I want to be touched; I don't want to be shocked into shame of being human and rejected through all possible theater tricks of a non-theater; I don't mind being whipped again from the stage—since I seek experience, not escape—but I want to feel the warmth of the human hand that cracks the whip. I want to feel, by whatever implications, that there is excitement in mere existence and beauty in being.

Theater is imagined reality, even if you leave the body to decide its own sequence of action or if you maintain that anything can follow anything or if you let the dancing body dis-

Jeff Duncan performing the solo "Panic" from *Anna Sokolow*'s
Rooms, a masterpiece of the American modern dance, drama-
tizes man's struggles, fears, and helplessness in an existentialist
world

Photo by Edward Effron; courtesy of Jeff Duncan

cover its own momentum of automatic movement or if you try to reduce every movement, every experience translated into a dance, to its purest essence and skeleton-like truth. What I then demand from the creative artist is that the sequence of movement has meaning in terms of imagery that transcends reality. One may give chance its chance and say with Wallace Stevens: "A poem need not have meaning and like most things in nature often does not have." But the crux of the matter remains the magic of an imagined world—no matter which form it takes—that communicates in terms of visual images, powerfully new and impressive enough to elope with my own imagination.

The search for the identity of man in his time, the propelling force with which the modern dance began, will always be the task of the dancer-choreographer. He will have to find an idiom which is neither representational nor non-theater, neither literal nor detached from existence. He may shape strange creatures of magic. Theater is magic. He may, with cruel consciousness, create movement imagery that has inherent dramatic power. He may turn to the past or communicate the problems of contemporary life. What matters is the immediacy of some sort of truth, even if the truth may lie in the denial that the modern artist should give *meaning*. But as long as movement, shape, form, color communicate, their artistic totality cannot help evoking associations in our minds.

The value of any work of art lies in its truth, its inner truth. It only exists when it speaks to us in a language which we do not necessarily have to understand, but which strikes a chord in our being, which relates and helps us find our self. This truth may have many forms and fashions of expression and certainly lies not only in a legible message, it must be a bridge of understanding, however open to interpretation. Finally, any work of art reveals itself through its mystery, through that ultimate intangible something which proves that creation is a secret, the key to which we lose while seeking it.

There is something unmistakable about a work of art. When later generations look at us they will not see the feeble, defiant scribble on the wall, "Kilroy was here," and mistake it for art. They must see an image of a danced reality, an image, formed out of an inner cry and the outer chaos, and feel that the Creator must have passed by.

I fully realize that experimentation is basic to all arts which cannot help growing beyond themselves from time to time, that is from each time-bound period to the next, because standstill is death and every growing process demands the new face of its epoch. What so often creates confusion in the mind of our contemporary artists is their desperate notion that they must start "from scratch." But we cannot. Paul Klee did not when he fled into the rich, unspoiled world of the child's imagination, nor did Picasso when he began as a classicist and then went back to the mask image of primitive man with a cubist squint in his eye. However, every period feels more akin to one that has preceded it and will, of its own necessity, start from there with the wisdom and dream of its own age.

As we have succeeded in reducing our artistic expression to a provocative nothingness, I see the potential of an almost classic cleanness and a form-fulfilled, architectural lightness in our future attempts at recreating the image of our age characterized by cosmic penetration. And since there is an inherent romantic touch to our scientific flight into the unknown, to modern man's almost dream-fulfilled existence in which everything he can think of will be at his command, I would not be surprised to see the twentieth-century classicism followed or rather paralleled and fought by—knowing the artists as I do—a very scientifically indoctrinated neo-romanticism. And then later history books may note briefly the long period of confusing isms and chaotic issues (1917–67) through which modern man staggered, stunned by his own powerfulness and greatness, and after which he slowly found himself again in humble realization of his own beauty-embracing, poetic potentialities and of the many truths in the final truth of his lasting limitations as man and artist.

Biographical Notes

FREDERICK ASHTON: Born September 17, 1906, at Guayaquil, Ecuador. Studied dancing under Massine, Lipinska, and Rambert. Choreographed for Ballet Rambert, Sadler's Wells Ballet, Royal Ballet, and Royal Danish Ballet. Director of Royal Ballet, London. Best known ballets: *Façade, Checkmate, A Wedding Bouquet, Cinderella, Illuminations, Ondine, Marguerite and Armand, Romeo and Juliet.*

GEORGE BALANCHINE: As a youth, before leaving Russia at the age of twenty, choreographed a number of works. Began to choreograph for Diaghilev in 1925: *La Chatte, Apollo, Prodigal Son.* Founded Ballets 1933 in Paris, came to the United States in 1934 and, from then on, has worked mainly with Lincoln Kirstein as a teacher of the School of American Ballet and as a choreographer for The American Ballet, Ballet Theatre, Ballet Russe de Monte Carlo, Ballet Society, Metropolitan Opera Ballet, and The New York City Ballet. One of the most prolific choreographers who also choreographed musicals on Broadway, films as well as television ballets. Best known for: *Apollo, Orpheus, La Valse, The Four Temperaments, Symphony in C, Firebird, The Nutcracker, Ivesiana, Seven Deadly Sins, Episodes, Liebeslieder Walzer, A Midsummer Night's Dream, Don Quixote, Movements for Piano and Orchestra.*

CLIVE BARNES: Born in London, England, 1927. After a false start as medical student at London University, became dance critic. Has written for: *Dance and Dancers, The New Statesman and Nation, Daily Express, Spectator,* etc. Became London correspondent for *Dance Magazine* while chief writer on dance for the *Times* (London). Began to cover European dance events for the New York *Times* in 1963 and became its New York dance critic in the fall of 1965. Publications: *Ballet in Britain Since the War* (1952), *Frederick Ashton and His Ballets* (Dance Perspectives, 1961), co-author of *Ballet Here and Now* (1961). Contributor to many magazines, among them *The New Republic* and *Life.* Was once executive editor of both *Plays and Players, Music and Musicians.*

SELMA JEANNE COHEN: Born in Chicago. Studied ballet and modern. Graduate of the University of Chicago, Ph.D. (English). Taught English at several universities and dance history at the School of Performing Arts, Connecticut College School of Dance. Contributed to *Dance Magazine, Dance News, Saturday Review, Kenyon Review, New York Times*, etc. Books for the New York Public Library: *Famed for Dance* (1960), *Stravinsky and the Dance* (1962). Editor of *The Modern Dance: Seven Statements of Belief* (Wesleyan, 1966). Co-editor of *Dance Perspectives* (1959–65), editor from 1965.

BIRGIT CULLBERG: Studied with Kurt Jooss, later ballet and Graham technique. Has worked for many internationally known companies, among them Opera Ballet in Stockholm, Royal Danish Ballet, The New York City Ballet, The American Ballet Theatre. Best known for: *Miss Julie, Medea, Lady from the Sea, Dionysus*. Has several television ballets to her credit; choreographed ballet for *Tannhaeuser* in Bayreuth (1965).

ANGNA ENTERS: Mime, dancer, playwright, painter, novelist and essayist. Born in New York. Awarded two Guggenheim Fellowships (1934, 1935). Famous for her mime creations, such as *Boy Cardinal, Auto da Fé, Pavana, Artist's Life*. Plays: *Love Possessed Juana* (1946), *The Unknown Lover* (1947), both produced Houston Little Theatre. Artist in residence and director (Dallas City Center), artist in residence at Baylor University, Fellow for Advanced Studies at Wesleyan University. Publications: *First Person Plural* (1937), *Silly Girl* (1944), *Among the Daughters* (1954), *Artist's Life* (1958), *On Mime* (1965). Exhibited in London, New York, and at several universities in the United States.

ERICK HAWKINS: Born in Trinidad, Colorado. Was graduated from Harvard, with concentration in Greek literature and art. First dance study was with Harald Kreutzberg, Salzburg; first choreography, *Show Piece*, for Ballet Caravan, New York. First starring role partner to Martha Graham in her *American Document*; created the principal male roles in most of her dances for twelve years. Concurrently, gave his first solo concert in New York in 1942, which premiered such dances as his *Yankee Bluebritches*. Was also seen in the leading role in Agnes de Mille's *Oklahoma!* In 1951 began collaboration with composer Lucia Dlugoszewski and sculptor-designer Ralph Dorazio, which has continued until the present. First work of this collaboration was *openings of the (eye)*. Another work, program-length, *Here and Now With Watchers* (1957). Danced with his company at the Théâtre des Nations Festival in Paris (1963): *Cantilever, 8 Clear Places, Geography of Noon*. Works premiered in 1965: *Lords of Persia* and *Naked Leopard*.

HANYA HOLM: Leading American dancer, choreographer, and teacher in modern dance. Born and educated in Germany, joined the Mary Wigman School, co-director and chief instructor at Wigman Institute for ten years. Came to New York in 1931 to found the New York Mary Wigman School, known as Hanya Holm Studio since 1936. New York debut with *Trend* (1937). Directed, taught, and produced modern dance creations at the Colorado Springs Fine Arts Center since 1941. Has choreographed for all media including film and television. Best known for her Broadway shows: *The Eccentricities of Davy Crockett (Ballet Ballads), The Insect Comedy, Kiss Me, Kate, My Fair Lady, Camelot*. Staged opera and plays.

DORIS HUMPHREY: One of the leading dancers and choreographers of modern dance. Was a featured soloist with Denishawn, joined forces with Charles Weidman in 1928; sickness interrupted her dancing career in 1945. Guggenheim Fellowship (1949). Was artistic director for the José Limón Company from 1946 on. Her major works are: *The Shakers, Passacaglia, Theatre Piece, Day on Earth, Lament for Ignacio Sanchez Mejias, Night Spell, Ruins and Visions, Dawn in New York*. Her only book and last will, *The Art of Making Dances*, was published posthumously in 1959.

ANN HUTCHINSON: Born in New York City. Educated in Europe, started dance training at the Jooss-Leeder School in England. Studied with Martha Graham and other modern dancers and has since specialized in ballet. Co-founder and honorary president of the Dance Notation Bureau in New York, author of the definitive textbook, *Labanotation* (1954), leading authority on systems of dance notation and movement research.

GEORGE JACKSON: Born in Vienna, studied at the University of Chicago, now lives in New York. Has worked on and published in literary, dance, and scientific magazines here and abroad. The essay included in this volumn was daydreamed in August, 1963, while on a biological expedition into the Amazon Jungle. Its title refers to Heinrich von Kleist's dialogue *Über das Marionettentheater*.

PAULINE KONER: Combines the spirit of modernity with unlimited technique, gained through her early association with Fokine. Now known as one of the leading modern dancers. Has appeared in almost all countries of the world, including Russia and Japan. Was featured guest artist with the José Limón Company for fifteen years. Famous for solo dances, among which *Farewell* is one of her most outstanding achievements. Received the *Dance Magazine* Award in 1964. Was invited by the Fulbright Commission to go to Japan to perform, lecture, and establish a workshop for the Japanese modern dance. Has taught at many schools and colleges.

RUDOLF LABAN: One of the greatest theorists of movement in general and the modern dance in particular. Extended his studies from the theater to the working problems, the stresses and strains involved in the various occupations. Lived in England during and after the Second World War. Among his early pupils were Mary Wigman and Kurt Jooss. Has written several books: *Effort* (1947), *Modern Educational Dance* (1948), *The Mastery of Movement on the Stage* (1950). Best known as the creator of *Labanotation*.

JOSÉ LIMÓN: Born in Mexico, moved to California in his youth where he went to school. Later in New York, joined the Humphrey-Weidman group. In 1946 founded his own company which was under Doris Humphrey's artistic direction until her death. Has taught at Bennington College, Sarah Lawrence College, Connecticut College School of Dance, and at the Dance Department of Juilliard. Best known for: *The Moor's Pavane, La Malinche, The Traitor, There Is A Time,* and *Missa Brevis.*

NORMAN LLOYD: Born in 1909. Studied at New York University and holds several awards. Taught at many schools, among them Sarah Lawrence College, Juilliard School of Music (1946–63), dean of Oberlin Conservatory of Music (1963–65). Now director for Arts, The Rockefeller Foundation. Has been closely associated with the modern dance movement as a composer and conductor of dance scores for Martha Graham, Hanya Holm, Doris Humphrey, José Limón, Anna Sokolow, and Charles Weidman. Among his publications: *Fireside Book of Folksongs* (1947), *New Golden Song Book* (1962), *Fireside Book of Favorite American Songs* (1952).

CARMELITA MARACCI: Born in Montevideo, Uruguay. Grew up in San Francisco. Although her ballet technique was exquisite, she refused to be a ballerina. Had a superb command of the Spanish style and yet declined to be a Spanish dancer. She is a born rebel and has perfected dances of exuberant gaiety, barbed satire, and deep tragedy. Now teaching in Los Angeles.

MERLE MARSICANO: Born in Philadelphia. Danced with Mikhail Mordkin when she was still a child. Studied Spanish dancing as well as modern; took composition classes with Louis Horst while studying with Martha Graham. Later broke away from the representational school of the modern dance. Settled in New York City, gave many recitals at Henry Street Playhouse and at the "Y" Lexington Avenue. For many years she was a solo dancer and is now working with a group. Best known for: *Figure of Memory, Passage, Three Dances, The Long Gallery.*

JOHN MARTIN: Dean of American dance critics, was the most influential voice when the rebels of the modern dance started out to find themselves artistically. Was critic of the New York *Times* which he

joined in 1927 for more than thirty years. Lectured and taught at
many schools, colleges, and universities. Publications: *The Modern
Dance* (1936), *Introduction to the Dance* (1939), *The Dance*
(1946, revised edition 1963), *World Book of Modern Ballet* (1952).
Contributed to many magazines, such as *Dance Index* and *Saturday
Review*.

DONALD McKAYLE: Born and raised in New York City, began his
dance career while a student at the College of the City of New
York. Became a member of the New Dance Group and their company under the direction of Jane Dudley, Sophie Maslow, and
William Bales. Continued his studies with Martha Graham, Hadas-
sah, and Pearl Primus, performed as a major soloist in the companies
of Jean Erdman, Merce Cunningham, Martha Graham, Anna Sokolow. Formed his own company in 1951 and created *Games, Rainbow
'Round My Shoulder, District Storyville* among others. Choreographed many television shows and on Broadway *Golden Boy, A
Time for Singing*, directed off-Broadway *Trumpets of the Lord*, and
choreographed for the New York Shakespeare Festival *The Tempest*
and *As You Like It*. His ballets are also in repertoire of the Bat-Sheva
Company of Israel and the Harkness Ballet of New York.

LA MERI: Born in Louisville, Kentucky, but part of childhood spent
in San Antonio, Texas. Proximity to the Mexican border is doubtless
responsible for her interest in exotic peoples, although her poetry
shows an early interest in folklore. Named after her father Russell
Meriwether Hughes, she changed her name to La Meri after an
engagement in Mexico City. Danced her way around the world after
her debut as a concert dancer in 1928 in New York. One of the most
famous dancers in the ethnological field. Author of seven books of
poetry and four books on the dance: *Dance As an Art Form* (1935),
Spanish Dancing (1948), *The Dance* (1931), *Gesture Language of
the Hindu Dance* (1942).

ALWIN NIKOLAIS: Born in Southington, Connecticut. At sixteen was
a professional musician. Was attracted to dance after seeing Mary

Wigman perform. Studied with the foremost American modern dancers. First choreography was a commission from the Wadsworth Atheneum in 1940, *Eight Column Line* with music by Ernst Krenek. In 1948 he was appointed co-director of the Henry Street Settlement Playhouse in New York City where he has established a school and company. His unique kind of dance theater began in 1953 with *Village of Whispers*. His work received acclaim in 1956 with *Kaleidoscope*. It was followed by a full evening theater piece each year including among others *Prism, The Bewitched, Allegory, Totem, Imago, Sanctum* and *Galaxy. Vaudeville of the Elements* was commissioned by the Walker Art Foundation for the new Tyrone Guthrie Theatre in Minneapolis (1965). His work has been televised in the United States, Canada, and Europe. Creates all aspects of his theater: choreography, costumes, lighting, and electronic sound score uniting them into one full theatrical event.

YVONNE RAINER: Born in San Francisco. Came to New York City in 1956. Studied with Edith Stephen, Sevilla Fort (ethnic), and Martha Graham as well as Lisan Kay (ballet). Worked with Ann Halprin in the summer of 1960. Started to choreograph in 1960 while working with Robert Dunn at the Cunningham School. Danced with James Waring, Beverly Schmidt, Aileen Passloff, and Judith Dunn. Since 1962 has been connected with the dancers of the Judson Memorial Church and created several works which were called stunning and controversial. Appeared at the Modern Museum in Stockholm in 1964, and also in London; in Ann Arbor, Michigan, at the Festival of the Arts in Buffalo, Boston, Richmond, and Hartford (Wadsworth Atheneum).

KURT SELIGMANN: Has exhibited his works in almost all the great cities of the world; leading surrealist painter; came to New York from Paris in 1939; regular exhibits in New York, Chicago, Mexico, and other places. Designed the costumes and stage sets for ballets done by Balanchine and Hanya Holm; lectured at the Briarcliff Junior College, Columbia University, and High School of Music and Art, New York. Interested in Black Magic and wrote a book published by Pantheon on this subject.

WALTER SORELL: Born in Vienna. Studied at the University of Vienna and Columbia University. Teaches at Columbia University and The New School, has guest-lectured at many colleges. Drama editor of *The Cresset* (Valparaiso University), contributing editor of *Dance Magazine*, was editor of *Dance Observer* (1959–64). Contributed to *Saturday Review*, *Vogue*, *Esquire*, *Opera News*, *Shakespeare Quarterly*, *America Illustrated*, etc. Translated books by Goethe, Hesse, Remarque, and others, also Mary Wigman's *The Language of Dance*. Publications: *The Dance Has Many Faces* (1951); forthcoming publications: *The Story of the Human Hand*, *Dance. A Chronicle*, *Jean Cocteau*. Plays: *Everyman Today*, *Isadora Duncan*, *The Flowering of a Barren Fig Tree*, *Olivia and a Dream*, *The End of the Tether*. Several television plays.

RUTH ST. DENIS: Born in Newark, New Jersey. First theatrical engagement in David Belasco's American version of *Zaza*. At the end of five years in various Belasco companies, she was attracted toward the Orient. Solo career as an Oriental dancer extended roughly from 1906 to 1914, when she met Ted Shawn. They combined their talents in the school of Denishawn. Eventually built Denishawn House in the upper reaches of New York City, through whose portals went forth many who now bear distinguished names in the world of the dance: Martha Graham and Doris Humphrey, Charles Weidman and Jack Cole. The main inspiration for the "sacred dance" movement in America. Capezio Dance Award (1961). Devoted her life to the fulfillment of the spiritualizing of the arts in America. Has lectured and written poetry and essays. Her autobiography, *My Unfinished Life*, was published in 1940.

HELEN TAMIRIS: Dancer and choreographer, studied with Metropolitan Opera Ballet and Fokine, danced with Metropolitan Opera three seasons, toured South America as ballerina. Made concert debut in New York in 1927. Introduced American folk and Negro spirituals at Salzburg Festival. Danced in Berlin and Paris. Founded her first company in 1930, organized Dance Repertory Theater (1930–31). Choreographed many musicals: *It's Up To You* (1943),

Up In Central Park (1945), *Show Boat* (1946), *Annie Get Your Gun* (1946), *Inside U.S.A.* (1948), *Touch and Go* (1949), *Bless You All* (1950), *Fanny* (1954), *Plain and Fancy* (1955). Created *Dance of Walt Whitman* in 1953, founded her second company in 1959 in which year she choreographed *Memoir*, followed by *Women Song, Once Upon a Time, Rituals, Versus*.

WALTER TERRY: Born in Brooklyn, New York, in 1913. Studied with many notable dancers and teachers. Became dance critic: Boston *Herald* (1936–39), New York *Herald Tribune* (1939–42). Served in U.S. Army Air Corps, master sergeant (1942–45). Professor of Dance, Adelphi College (1941); American University, Cairo, Egypt (1944–45). Principal dancer, *Rose Marie*, Royal Opera House, Cairo (1943–44). Currently dance critic, New York *Herald Tribune* (since October, 1945). Contributed to many dance magazines and published *Invitation to Dance* (1941), *Star Performance* (1954), *Ballet in Action* (with Paul Himmel, 1954), *The Dance in America* (1956), *Ballet: A New Guide to the Liveliest Art* (1959), *On Pointe!: The Story of Dancing* (1962), *Isadora Duncan* (1963). For several years was dance editor of the *Encyclopaedia Britannica*, lectured extensively, and is currently at work on a biography of Ruth St. Denis.

CHARLES WEIDMAN: Born in Lincoln, Nebraska, in 1901. Member of Denishawn company for eight years, first professional experience in vaudeville (*Xochitl* with Martha Graham). Established school and concert company with Doris Humphrey (1927). Taught at several colleges. Choreographed *Traditions, The Happy Hypocrite, Quest, Candide, Flickers, Daddy Was A Fireman, A House Divided*, and has become famous for his interpretation of James Thurber's *Fables*.

Selected Reading Guide

Amberg, George. *Ballet in America*. New York, Duell, 1949 (also published under the title *Ballet*. Mentor Books, New American Library, 1949).

Ambrose, Kay. *Classical Dances and Costumes of India*. London, Black, 1950.

Balanchine, George. *Complete Stories of Great Ballets*. Garden City, N.Y., Doubleday, 1954.

Benedict, Ruth. *Patterns of Culture*. Boston, Houghton Mifflin, 1934.

Boaz, Franziska. *The Function of Dance in Human Society*. New York, The Boaz School, 1944.

Bowers, Faubion. *The Dance of India*. New York, Columbia University Press, 1953.

—— *Theatre in the East*. New York, Nelson, 1956.

Chujoy, Anatole, and P. W. Manchester. *Dance Encyclopedia*. New York, Barnes, 1949. New edition, Simon and Schuster, 1966.

Duncan, Isadora. *Art of the Dance*. New York, Theatre Arts, 1928.

—— *My Life*. New York, Liveright, 1927.

Ellis, Havelock. *Dance of Life*. Boston, Houghton Mifflin, 1923.

Ernst, Earle. *The Kabuki Theatre*. New York, Oxford University Press, 1956.

Gopal, Ram. *Indian Dancing*. London, Phoenix House, 1951.

Fokine, Vitale. *Fokine. Memoirs of a Ballet Master*. Boston, Little, Brown, 1961.

Fraser, Sir John. *The Golden Bough*. New York, Macmillan, 1947.

Haskell, Arnold. *Ballet*. New York, Famous Books, 1938; rev. ed., New York, Pelican Books, 1949.

—— *Diaghileff*. London, Gollancz, 1935.

H'Doubler, Margaret. *Dance—A Creative Art Experience*. New York, Crofts, 1940.

Hering, Doris, ed. *Twenty-Five Years of American Dance*. New York, Orthwine, 1951.

Horst, Louis. *Pre-Classic Dance Forms*. New York, Kamin Dance Publishers, 1953.

——*Modern Dance Forms*. San Francisco, Impulse Publications, 1961.

Humphrey, Doris. *The Art of Making Dances*. New York, Holt, Rinehart and Winston, 1959.

Hutchinson, Ann. *Labanotation*. New York, New Directions, 1954.

Kirstein, Lincoln. *Dance*. New York, Putnam, 1935.

Laban, Rudolf. *The Mastery of Movement*. London, MacDonald and Evans, 1950.

Langer, Susanne. *Feeling and Form*. New York, Scribner's, 1953.

Lloyd, Margaret. *The Borzoi Book of Modern Dance*. New York, Knopf, 1949.

Love, Paul. *Modern Dance Terminology*. New York, Kamin, 1953.

Magriel, Paul David. *Chronicles of the American Dance*. New York, Henry Holt, 1948.

Martin, John. *The Modern Dance*. Brooklyn, Dance Horizons, 1965. Original edition, A. S. Barnes, 1933.

——*Introduction to the Dance*. Brooklyn, Dance Horizons, 1965. Original edition, W. W. Norton, 1939.

Moore, Lillian. *Artists of the Dance*. New York, Crowell, 1938.

Nettl, Paul. *The Story of Dance Music*. New York, Philosophical Library, 1947.

Nicoll, Allardyce. *The Development of the Theatre*. 4th ed., rev.; New York, Harcourt, Brace, 1957. Original edition, 1927.

Noverre, Jean Georges. *Letters on Dancing and Ballet*. London, Beaumont, 1951.

Palmer, Winthrop. *Theatrical Dancing in America*. New York, Ackerman, 1945.

Sachs, Curt. *World History of the Dance*. New York, W. W. Norton, 1937.

St. Denis, Ruth. *My Unfinished Life*. New York, Harper, 1939.

Shawn, Ted. *Every Little Movement*. New York, Ted Shawn, 1954.

Tabourot, Jehan. *Orchesography*. London, Beaumont, 1925. New edition; Brooklyn, Dance Horizons, 1965.

Terry, Walter. *The Dance in America*. New York, Harper, 1956.

Valery, Paul. *Dance and the Soul*. London, J. Lehmann, 1951. In *Selected Writings*. New York, New Directions, 1950.

INDEX

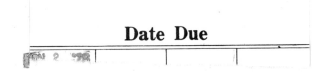

Date Due